CREATING

TeXTURE

WITH

TeXTILES!

LINDA F. MCGEHEE

Krause Publications

700 East State St., Iola, WI 54990-0001
Telephone 715-445-2214
www.krause.com

Please call or write for our free catalog of publications. Our toll-free number to place an order or obtain a free catalog is 800-258-0929 or please use our regular business telephone 715-445-2214 for editorial comment and further information.

Book design by Jan Wojtech
Photography by Scot R. Smith, Smith Photographic Services

Manufactured in the United States of America

This book was written to inspire creativity in the use of textiles, different forms of embellishment, and manipulation of fabric. Each project highlights different techniques, which will hopefully excite the reader to begin exploring texture with textiles. No responsibility can be taken for results due to varying materials and procedures and results cannot be assured.

Library of Congress Cataloging-In-Publication Data

McGehee, Linda F.
Creating Texture with Textiles

1. Sewing   2. Fabric   3. Title

ISBN 0-87341-657-0
CIP 98-84108

Acknowledgments

Nothing worthwhile is accomplished without the support of others. A thread is nothing without a needle and fabric. A needle needs motivation and direction. I need a sewing machine. It's this ongoing process of collection and dependency on others that has allowed me to create this book. I wish to thank those who have been involved by supplying products and equipment.

Sewing Machines and Accessories: Baby Lock USA, Bernina of America, Inc., Brother International, Elna USA, The New Home Sewing Machine Co., Pfaff American Sales Corp., Singer, and Viking Sewing Machine Inc.

Batting and Interfacing: Fairfield Processing Corp., HTC-Handler Textile Corp., Mountain Mist, Morning Glory, Staple Aids Sewing Corp., and The Warm Co.

Buttons: Albe Creations, Inc., JHB International, Inc., J-J Handworks by Jane Schreven, and mamamania-vintage buttons.

Cutting Equipment: Omnigrid, Inc., and June Taylor, Inc.

Dyes: Cache Junction Seitec.

Fabrics: Benartex, Inc., Capitol Imports, Inc. of Tallahassee, Cherrywood Fabrics, Inc., Dyenamics Hand Dyed Fabrics, Hi Fashion, Inc., Hoffman California Fabrics, Maywood Studio, P&B Fabrics, John Kaldor Fabricmaker USA Ltd., Robert Kaufman Co. Inc., Moda Fabrics, and Quilters Only Springs Industries, Inc.

Threads: Coats & Clark, Inc., Gutermann of America, Inc., Kreinik Mfg. Co. Inc., Madeira, Mettler Threads, Sulky of America, and YLI Corp.

Needles: Schmetz.

Iron: Rowenta.

I am grateful to my students who have accepted my ideas and knowledge and asked for more; to the stores who continue to promote and sell my patterns, books, and other products; and to my colleagues in the industry who have enlightened me with questions and answers.

My special thanks to Barbara, my editor, who patiently worked with me while things slowly trickled in, and who made my puzzle pieces of photos and copy look absolutely wonderful in book form.

Many thanks to my fantastic staff at Ghee's who have proofed, manned the shop, and stood by me through hills and valleys.

My very special thanks to my sweetheart Jack, who patiently proofed and pre-edited when I know there were other things he wanted to do; who listened to and didn't complain about the hum of the machine in the wee hours of the night or wakening hours of the morning; who holds me, scolds me, and fills me with nourishment.

My thanks to each of you for helping to make my life fun while enabling me to follow my dreams.

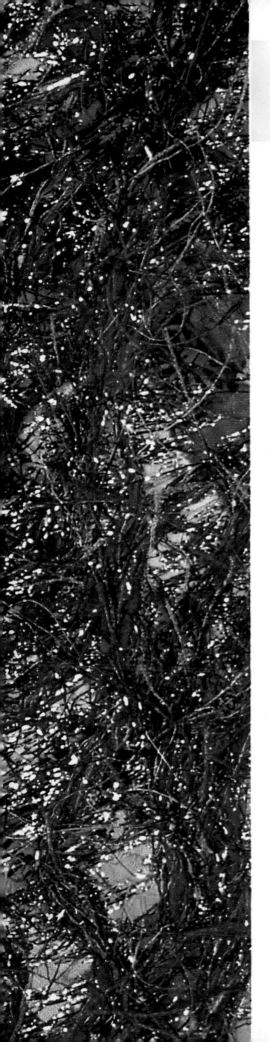

Introduction

Sewing has changed drastically in recent years. Sewing machines are incredible with their vast selection of decorative and utility stitches. Their ability to duplicate stitching which at one time was solely handwork expedites processes. There are specialized sewing machine feet to make tasks easy and accurate. It's a whole new ball game.

The enormous selection of thread types and colors make any project an adventure. The base begins with a wide range of fabrics.

In the sewing techniques I describe in this book, as in nature, nothing is perfect and everything is perfect. The fabric can be manipulated in unorthodox ways and still be beautiful.

Enjoy a new freedom of sewing crooked and working with wrinkled fabric. Slice and dice fabric, then sew it back together again. Treat fabric and thread like an artist uses canvas and paint. The sky is the limit. With a few guidelines, some basic information, and unleashed freedom, sewing becomes an art form.

Remember, there are no set rules. The possibilities are endless. Experiment with designs, threads, and fabrics. Discover other techniques. Enjoy new freedom with the sewing machine.

You never know the outcome until you play the game. Enjoy a new adventure using your machine and all the toys that go along with it. Expand your horizons by experimenting with texture. Use equipment and accessories that will make it easier to explore new applications. Play with all the wonderful fabrics, threads, yarns, laces and trims that are available today.

Lighten up. Let the creative juices flow. Find out how creative you really are. Enjoy the ride.

Linda

Table of Contents

Chapter 1

Interesting Words and Phrases

Every vocation, avocation, and group activity of any kind develops a vocabulary unique to its particular activity. In working with textures and fabrics, there are many such words that have a special interpretation. To be clear and avoid misunderstanding, here is a glossary of some words and phrases used in the following pages.

Appliqué: A design applied to the surface of another fabric using hand or machine stitching, glue, or fusing. To apply designs to the surface of another fabric.

Batiste: A fine, sheer fabric of plain weave made of various fibers, usually cotton.

Batting: A thin to fluffy layer of natural or synthetic non-woven fibers used between layers of fabric to give soft support for quilting.

Bead: A small shaped piece of hard material pierced for threading with others on a string or wire, or for sewing on fabrics.

Beading (with beads): A decoration with beads.

Bias: A diagonal line other than the lengthwise or crossgrain of fabric. True bias makes a 45° angle across the lengthwise and crossgrain. It has greater stretch and give and ravels less than any other cut edge.

Bobbin Thread: Thread designed to use specifically in the bobbin when decorative thread is used in the needle. This thread is lighter weight and is not designed for garment construction.

Butt: To push together so the edges meet and just touch rather than overlap, as in combining laces and embroidery trims in heirloom sewing.

Colorfast: Fabric that keeps its original color without fading or running during cleaning or laundering as long as the manufacturer's instructions are followed.

Collection: Something gathered or assembled into a mass or pile. An accumulation gathered for a hobby, as in stamps, coins, books, fabric, or thread. These items can be necessary or an indulgence.

Continuous Bias: Continuing without a break. An unbroken or uncut strip of fabric cut on the diagonal or bias grain of the fabric.

Corded Piping: A narrow fold of fabric filled with cord used for trimming seams to add dimension and definition.

Couching: A method of embroidery where a design is created by hand or machine stitching over threads, cords, braids, or yarns that have been laid on the surface of a fabric.

Crinkle: To make or become wrinkled. Crease, roughen, crumble, ripple, fold, crimp.

Crossgrain: The threads or yarns running across a fabric from selvage to selvage.

Cutting Mat: The cutting surface necessary when using a rotary cutter to avoid marring the table and damaging the cutting blade.

Embroidery Beading: A hemstitch with slits, through which ribbons can be laced.

Entredeux: An embroidery trim used between two laces or embroideries to connect and add strength.

Fashion Fabric: Fabric visible on the finished project. It is not necessarily the side of the fabric designed to be the right side. Sometimes the wrong side is more pleasing to the eye or adds better contrast.

Filler: The predominant color of fabric used repeatedly in a set. The fabric used to fill in and complete the set.

Fleece: Any of various soft or woolly battings sold by the yard used for underlining.

Fusible: The resin coating on the back of interfacing used to join or bond to fabric by applying heat and moisture. A web-like material that melts when heat is applied. Refer to the manufacturer's instructions—applications of heat, moisture, and time may vary.

Gimpe: An ornamental flat braid or round cord used as a trimming or filling.

Grain of Fabric: The warp or lengthwise threads or yarns of a fabric parallel to the selvage.

Heading: The straight, selvage edge of lace.

Heirloom Sewing: Converts French hand sewing to machine sewing methods using fine laces, trims, and fabrics to create a piece to be handed down in a family for generations.

Insertion: A lace or embroidery with two straight edges. The lace has heading on both sides; the embroidery has raw edges.

Interfacing: The fabric placed on the inside of a garment to give body, strength, and support. Interfacing is fusible or sew-in; knitted, woven, or non-woven; made of natural fibers or synthetic.

Need: Something useful, required, or desired that is lacking; state of extreme want as in fabric, thread, sewing equipment. Sometimes you need to indulge yourself.

Needle Position: On most machines, the position of the needle can be moved left or right of the center.

Needlepunch: A dense, non-woven sheet of polyester punched with thousands of polyester fibers sold by the yard for stuffing or stabilizing heavier projects like handbags.

Pearl Cotton or Rayon: Heavier thread used for crochet, filling, or couching.

Piping: A narrow fold of fabric for trimming seams to add dimension and definition.

Pintuck: A small flat fold stitched in a garment for ornamental or utility purposes. A stitch that produces tuck effects as a twin needle sews folds in the fabric.

Pivot: To turn the fabric with the needle inserted in the fabric to hold a position.

Presser Foot: The portion of the sewing machine that guards the needle and rests on the feed dogs, causing the machine to feed the fabric. There is a wide variety of presser feet available for various types of sewing. Each foot used in the processes described in this book are listed in the Foot Connection chapter.

Rip: To remove unwanted stitches. As ye sew, so shall ye rip. With so much decorative stitching and couching used on texture designs, there is less ripping than in conventional garment construction.

Rotary Cutter: A fabric-cutting device with a round blade attached to a handle resembling a pastry cutter.

As in any venture, there are many tips and tricks that make stitching more efficient. Throughout the book, these hints of special interest are designated with this symbol to emphasize information, help speed sewing time, and to guide you to professional results.

Ruler: A see-through measuring tool thick enough to use as a cutting edge with a straight edge and markings. My favorite ruler is 3″ to 4″ wide and 14″ to 20″ long with 1/4″ markings. Larger rules with 1/8″ grids are very awkward to work with.

Selvage: The finished edge that does not ravel on both sides of a woven fabric.

Set: Group of strips sewn together, usually 7″ to 15″ wide, intended for spiral piecing.

Shank: The part of a sewing machine needle opposite the eye that extends into the machine. The thread link between a button and fabric to allow for the thickness of the overlapping fabric.

Shoulder: The tapered portion of a sewing machine needle between the shank and shaft.

Sizing: A temporary fabric stiffener, much like starch, used in making fabric to improve the fabric's hand and appearance, providing body, weight, and luster. Sizing is removed by normal washing and care.

Spiraling: Winding upward from a center like the thread of a screw. Spiral piecing makes it simple to form larger diagonal strips from many narrow straight strips when a repeat is desired. This very efficient technique simplifies piecing with minimal fabric and time wasted. Though the process begins with the same procedure, the outcome will vary drastically when the sets are identical or varied, matched or unmatched.

Stash: The accumulation of fabrics, threads, trims, and sewing equipment acquired over time by saving and stowing.

Stitch and Flip: Assembling technique used to combine strips of fabric on a base such as muslin or batting where each added strip is sewn on the base and flipped before an additional strip is added.

Stitch in the Ditch: Technique of stitching inconspicuously on the right side of the fabric in a seamline.

Strip Piecing: Using strips of fabric to create piecing rather than working with templates or puzzle pieces.

Throat Plate: The flat portion of a sewing machine under the presser foot that covers the bobbin, protects the feed dogs and some inside working movements of a sewing machine.

Wick: The ability of fiber to carry moisture away from the body.

Chapter 2
THE FOOT CONNECTION

There is an assortment of sewing machine press-er feet available to make sewing easier, more accurate, and less stressful on the eyes and back. Ask your dealer for the presser feet that correspond to the techniques you are using. With the right feet, your sewing will be more precise and more fun. The following list includes presser feet I use constantly while sewing. Some of these feet may come with your sewing machine, others are additional accessories available through the dealer. Be sure to have the appropriate feet for the techniques you like to do.

Basic Stitching Foot: Commonly known as the all-purpose foot, the basic foot is used for most utility sewing from straight to zigzag stitching. The needle hole in the foot is wide to accommodate zigzag stitching which allows needle movement from the center position. This foot comes with every sewing machine.

Braiding Foot: A hole at the front of the foot is large enough to guide a small braid, heavier twisted threads, ribbon, yarn, or cord, making couching a simple embellishment.

Under the foot is a small groove that permits the bulk of the threads to pass without a buildup of stitches.

A simple zigzag or decorative stitch may be applied to hold the embellishing trims in position. Several sizes may be available for the same machine.

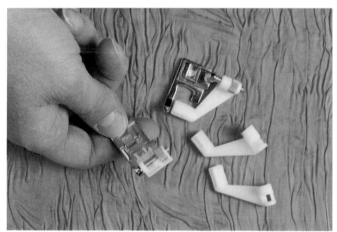

Button Sew-On Foot: This foot is used to hold buttons, snaps, and hooks and eyes in place while stitching with a zigzag stitch, making button sewing a breeze rather than a chore. Many feet have adjustable bars to sew shanks with ease. Another option to make a longer shank is a plastic adapter which holds the button up away from the fabric while stitching the button on the garment.

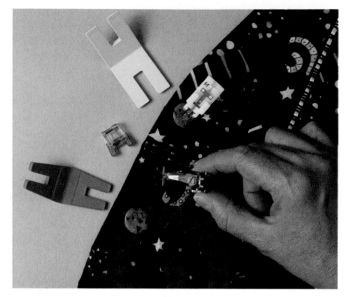

Creative Feet: Designed by a sewing expert for embellishment applications, these feet make sewing a breeze. The Satinedge™ Foot is for appliqué, top-stitching, and edgestitching. Sew 1/4″ sequins, ribbons, ric rac, and elastic with the Sequins 'N Ribbons™ Foot. And use the Pearls 'N Piping™ Foot for beads, pearls, corded piping, and decorative cords. These feet are generic feet available to fit most zigzag sewing machines. They are shown in the group photos with other feet.

Edgestitching or Joining Foot: Normally used to align the edge of fabric so the needle consistently stitches very close to the edge. Some feet have an adjustable guide to accommodate various widths, while others require changing the needle position.

This foot can be used to join laces and embroidery trims to each other or fabric in heirloom sewing.

This foot is efficient with some types of appliqué with ribbons or braids. A most versatile foot, the edge-stitching foot makes stitching in the ditch accurate and precise.

Fringe Foot: Designed for sewing thread fringe and faggoting, there is a metal lip extending upward on the foot.

When each stitch is formed, the lip allows the needle thread to make a loop rather than a flat stitch. As the machine continues to stitch, the loops fall off the back of the foot, forming a thread looped fringe.

Little Foot: Designed by a quilter for piecing, this foot is 1/4″ from the center needle position to the right edge, which creates an accurate 1/4″ seam allowance. Notches allow a perfect position for starting, stopping, and pivoting. The left side of the foot is 1/8″ from the center, allowing better control for easing curved piecing, miniatures, and stuffed animals or dolls. This foot attaches to most machines and is shown in the photo with the 1/4″ feet.

Multi-Hole or Groove Cording Foot: The different cording feet are used primarily to embroider several heavier threads or cords at once, resulting in a multicolored design much like a narrow ribbon.

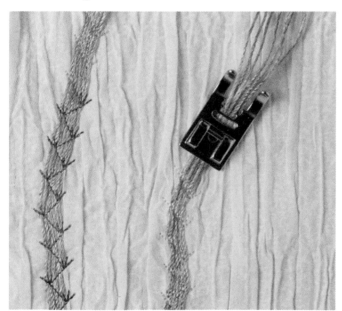

The different holes, grooves, or slots align the cords perfectly, keeping them in the same position while stitches form over the cords.

Practical or decorative stitches produce special effects. Other feet may have one to three holes or grooves used for the same purpose.

Open Toe Embroidery Foot: Intended for appliqué and embroidery, this foot has a small flat groove underneath, allowing the bulk of satin stitching threads to

pass to the back of the foot without a buildup of stitches.

The open toe permits excellent visibility of all curves and corners for accurate stitching. A double use for the foot is couching 1/4″ ribbon, ric rac, small braid, and sequins, which fit perfectly between the toes of the foot.

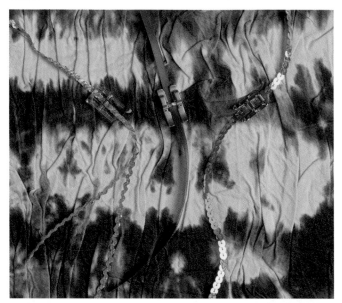

Pintuck Feet: Designed with a series of three to nine grooves underneath, these feet are used with a twin needle to produce perfect uniform tucks.

Consecutive parallel rows are stitched by placing the first tuck under one of the grooves in the foot.

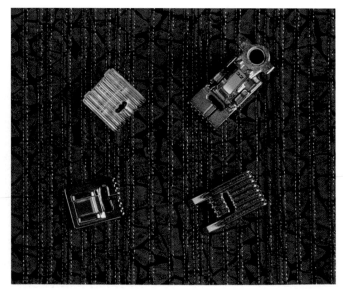

Larger grooved feet make larger tucks resembling traditional tucks.

Use different grooves in the foot or decorative stitches for special effects. Double check the stitch width on a decorative stitch to be certain the needle clears the hole in the presser foot. Different size needles combined with different grooved feet create tucks in a variety of sizes and make corded pintucks a breeze.

Larger grooved feet may be used to apply small corded piping.

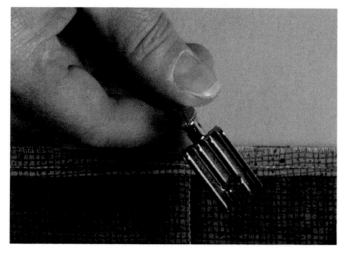

Piping or Beading Foot: Designed to make and apply corded piping, this foot contains a large hollowed groove on the bottom to facilitate heavier cords, beads, and pearls, allowing them to lie flat and glide easily along the bottom of the foot while being stitched in place. Adjust the needle position to the size cord or bead used.

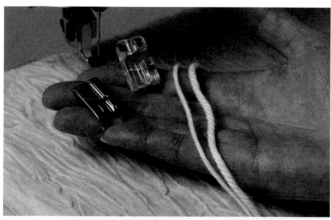

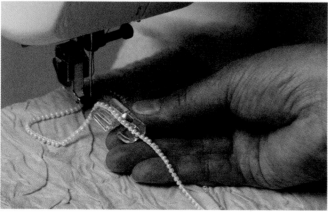

Teflon Foot: Similar in appearance to the basic foot from the upper side, this foot has a coating of Teflon on the bottom to allow non-slippery fabrics like suede and

plastic to glide under the foot rather than sticking to it.

Transparent Embroidery Foot: This foot looks very much like the open toe foot with the same features, except there is a transparent section before the needle hole. These two feet may be interchanged. Consider it a matter of preference.

1/4″ Foot: Designed for accuracy with patchwork, this foot has markings for perfect 1/4″ and 1/8″ seam allowances. Other markings on the foot permit precision corner pivoting as well as beginning and ending at the exact 1/4″ point. Excellent for 1/4″ topstitching too.

Chapter 3
Through the Eye of a Needle

The purpose of the sewing machine is to operate the needle. Do you remember those old needles? Then new technology allowed the development of numerous types of thread and improved needles were necessary to use the new threads. Different variations of fabric also required different needles. Add these to the modern sewing techniques and processess, and still other types of needles are required. The wide assortment of sewing machine needles available to accommodate the infinite variety of these different requirements causes confusion when it comes to selecting the correct and most efficient needle size and type for a given project.

To make selecting the proper needle type and size easier, refer to these guidelines. Many new needles have been introduced to accommodate the wide range of fabrics, threads, and techniques. To complete the task in the easiest and most timely manner, be certain to use the best needle for the purpose.

Needles are not designed to last forever. They must be changed frequently, usually every six to eight sewing hours. A needle becomes blunt from use as well as abuse. Sewing on buttons, charms, and beads improperly may shorten the life of a needle. Always sew with a good needle to prevent damage to the fabric and machine.

The numbering system on the needle packaging refers to the size of the needle. Not every type of needle is available in a wide variety of sizes, but the listing below will help you determine the correct size.

8/60 sheer fabrics, fine lace, silk
9/65 batiste, chiffon, organdy
10/70 crepe de chine, lawn, handkerchief linen
11/75 challis cotton knits, wool jersey
12/80 muslin, chintz, velvet, synthetic suede
14/90 textured linen, quilted fabrics, flannel
16/100 denim, sailcloth, fake fur, ticking
18/110 upholstery, canvas, drapery fabrics
19/120 work denim, very heavy fabrics

The American number (the first number) and European number (the number following the slash) are printed on the package cover. The smaller numbers (8/60 and 9/65) are used with lightweight fabrics, while the larger numbers (18/110 and 19/120) are used with heavier fabrics. The most common needle (12/80) is used for general sewing with medium weight fabric.

POINT OF INTEREST

THE UPPER PORTION OF SOME NEEDLE PACKAGING IS A MAGNIFIER TO ASSIST IN READING THE NEEDLE SIZE.

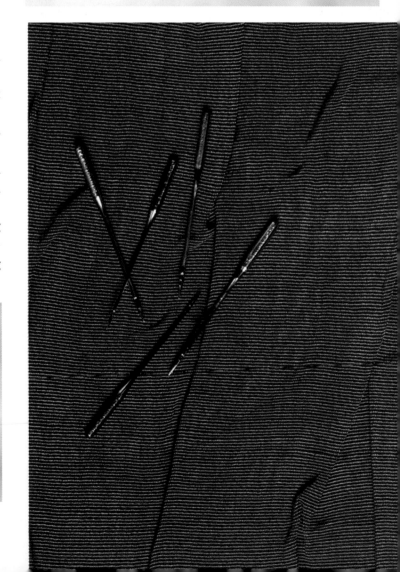

Ball Point Needles, with medium ball points, shift the fibers rather than pierce them, to avoid tiny holes on knitted fabrics.

Embroidery Needles feature a specially designed scarf and eye to eliminate skipped stitches and thread breakage with rayon threads. A red dot on the shoulder of the needle—that portion of the needle between the shank and shaft—differentiates the Embroidery Needle from other needles in the Schmetz needle line.

Jeans/Denim Needles, large size tapered sharp points, penetrate several layers of heavy denim weight or densely woven fabrics without breaking. They are suitable for sewing tapestry and other home decoration fabrics.

Leather Needles have a wedge-shaped point designed to penetrate leather, vinyl, and other plastic or non-woven material. Expect a permanent hole to remain in the fabric if the thread needs to be ripped out.

Metallica or Metafil Needles are designed with an elongated eye and special shaft to allow fragile metallic and lamé threads to pass, creating a more even fill of pattern stitches and eliminating skipped stitches or breakage.

Microtex/Sharps Needles, with tapered sharp points, are designed to penetrate silk and microfiber fabrics. They are best for topstitching and edgestitching perfectly straight stitches. A purple dot on the shoulder of the needle distinguishes the Microtex Needle from other needles in the Schmetz needle line.

Quilting Needles, with special tapered points, penetrate the layers of piecing and seaming in quilting or patchwork. A green dot on the shoulder of the needle is a distinguishing mark on Quilting Needles in the Schmetz line.

Self-Thread Machine Needles, general purpose needles, are helpful for persons who have difficulty threading regular machine needles. A small slot or opening at the side of the eye allows the thread to easily pass into the eye. The needle is weaker than normal machine needles.

Spring Embroidery Needles are designed for free motion embroidery stitching and quilting. Without a presser foot, the spring prevents the needle from drawing up the fabric, allowing the freedom to meander throughout the project. The needles are available in Universal for woven; Stretch for knits and elasticized fabrics; and Denim for heavy wovens.

Stretch Needles, with special construction, pass between fibers in the fabric rather than piercing them, making these needles suitable for synthetic suede and elastic knitwear fabrics, eliminating skipped stitches.

POINT OF INTEREST

DOUBLE AND TRIPLE NEEDLES ARE DESIGNED FOR ZIGZAG MACHINES THAT THREAD FRONT TO BACK.

Topstitch Needles have an extra large elongated eye and large groove in the shaft to allow buttonhole twist thread, two strands of all-purpose thread, or up to three strands of decorative thread to pass through the fabric without breaking or fraying.

Universal Point Needles are designed for both woven and knit fabric. The slight ball point makes this needle ideal for most garment construction.

Wing or Hemstitch Needles, which look like a serpent's head or wings, spread the fibers in the fabric to create holes as the design is stitched. Much like hemstitching in heirloom sewing, the needle can produce many special effects to resemble very tedious handwork.

Double Needles have two Universal needles with a crossbar attached to a single shank to allow two rows of perfectly parallel stitching. The first number on the

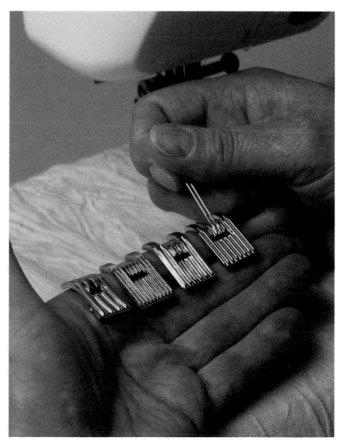

package with a decimal point refers to the distance between the two needles. The space can vary from 1.6, 2.0, 2.5, 3.0, 4.0, 6.0, to 8.0 mm. The second number refers to the needle size. These numbers—the distance between the two needles and the needle size—are printed on the crossbar for convenience. Not every type of double needle is available with a variety of space between the needles. Designed for pintucks and topstitching, the needle can be used for decorative stitching, depending on the distance between the needles and the opening of the throat plate on the machine. A single bobbin accommodates both needles.

Double Denim Needles with two denim needles, a crossbar, and a single shank, are ideal for topstitching and embellishing denims, tapestry, synthetic suede, and other closely woven fabrics.

Double Machine Embroidery Needles have two embroidery needles with a crossbar attached to a single shank. Use with metallic, rayon, and lamé threads.

Double Wing Needles have one Wing needle and one Universal needle with a crossbar attached to a single shank. The needle is designed to add interest to heirloom and other fine French sewing techniques.

Stretch Double Needles have two stretch needles with a crossbar attached to a single shank. They prevent skipped stitches and tiny holes in knit and stretch fabrics.

Triple Needles stitch three rows at a time instead of one or two. Three needles are attached to a crossbar and a single shank. The first number on the package with a decimal refers to the distance between the first and last needle. The second number refers to the size of the needle. Like the double needle, the triple needle is limited in stitch width decoration by the size of the opening in the throat plate.

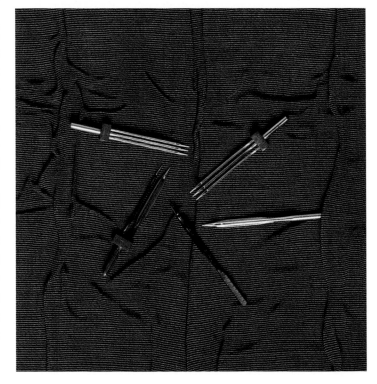

POINT OF INTEREST

WITH EMBELLISHMENT SEWING, YOU MAY FIND YOURSELF CHANGING THE NEEDLE FREQUENTLY FOR DIFFERENT TECHNIQUES. IF THE VARIETY OF NEEDLES SEEMS PUZZLING TO YOU, REMEMBER A FEW BASIC RULES.

A) CHOOSE THE NEEDLE POINT COMPATIBLE TO THE FABRIC.
B) CHOOSE THE NEEDLE SIZE ACCORDING TO THE WEIGHT OF THE FABRIC.
C) CHOOSE THE NEEDLE TYPE FOR THE DESIGN PURPOSE.

Some needle manufacturers color the shank or shoulder of the needle to avoid confusion after the needles are taken from the package.

Schmetz needles are labeled as follows:
- Embroidery Needles have a red dot on the shoulder;
- Microtex/Sharp Needles differentiate with a purple dot;
- Quilting Needles have a green distinguishing dot.

Anatomy of a Needle

The size of a needle is imprinted on the round side of the shank.

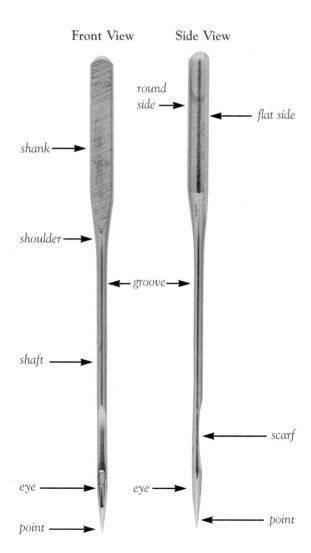

Front View   Side View

round side →   ← flat side

shank →

shoulder →

← groove →

shaft →

← scarf

eye →   eye →

point →   ← point

Chapter 4

Crinkling

CRINKLING: TO MAKE OR
  BECOME WRINKLED. CREASE,
  ROUGHEN, CRUMPLE, RIPPLE,
  FOLD, CRIMP.

My adventure with fabric began several years ago when broomstick skirts became a very important fashion item. I liked the look of the wrinkles. They added dimension and texture to fabric, giving it an entirely new appearance. However, I needed permanent wrinkles. I had no desire to twist and dry the fabric every time it was washed. Besides, I wanted to add other stitching and embellishments to the surface to completely change the base fabric. This would not work with a single layer of fabric. I needed to add something extra to hold the wrinkles in place.

This new fabric treatment evolved into crinkling. The twists, pleats, and tucks that occur when fabric is wet, gathered, twisted, dried, opened, and interfaced are the beginning of a wonderful adventure. The finished product is always a surprise. It is the beginning of the most fun creativity you can imagine. Enjoy the venture. The risks are minimal.

Types of Fabric

In experimenting with fabrics to crinkle, I have used just about every fabric known to man. Natural fabrics like cotton, linen, wool, and silk are wonderful to crinkle. They automatically make excellent wrinkles. Manmade fibers like sueded rayon, rayon velvet, rayon challis, and acetate moiré taffeta texture nicely with crinkling. Whether the fabrics are thin like handkerchief linen and sueded rayon or heavier like denim and cotton or rayon velvet, crinkling gives an extraordinary texture.

The only fabric that does not crinkle is polyester, which was designed not to wrinkle. No matter what the fabric content, any blend with polyester in it will not wrinkle. Therefore, don't attempt to use fabrics with polyester. It's a waste of time and energy.

Solid colors or predominantly solid-colored fabrics work nicely with crinkling. Many cotton fabrics available today are almost solid. There may be marbled, slightly shaded, muddled, or faded prints. Other fabrics have a color-on-color or a solid background with a very tiny print of one additional color, making it appear from a distance as if it were only one color. Stripes and plaids completely change in appearance with crinkling. They take on an undisciplined or uneven appearance. Additional threads, embellishments, and trims make a better showing on these solid background fabrics than on printed fabric. Don't avoid printed fabric, just be certain the print is not so large or bold that any trimming or embellishment is hidden with application.

How Much Fabric?

It is difficult to tell how much flat fabric is necessary to begin a project. With the crinkling process, there is very little fabric lost in length. The most shrinkage is in the width. To give a general idea of how much fabric to allow, plan to use one length for the front of a garment, one length for the back, and one length for each sleeve. This is a general rule. It may vary with the size and style of the garment.

One saying I like to remember is, "The best way to be creative is to start with less than you need." After all, isn't necessity the mother of invention? However, I change my mind so many times when starting a creative project, I feel better knowing I will have plenty of fabric. Allow extra whenever possible.

My Scottish background causes me to give a high priority to avoid wasting something as valuable as fabric. This has resulted in me cutting myself too short on fabric because I was trying to end up with the exact amount.

When I was in the seventh grade, I would purchase just enough fabric for a particular garment and proceed to sew it into that garment. Then when I had saved enough money from my baby-sitting work, I would purchase enough fabric for another garment and so on. I actually felt guilty about any leftovers. In the natural progression of things, I came upon a fabric that I liked very much but didn't have an immediate project in mind. I'm sure that at first I resisted the temptation to buy the coveted fabric, but at some point I finally succumbed and bought it. I indulged myself didn't I? Now,

years later, I have come to the realization that it's okay to own fabric with no immediate project or purpose. I encourage you to enjoy this luxury with knowledge and confidence that it doesn't make you a bad person. I firmly believe that once you shed your guilt and blossom into a fabric collector free of inhibitions, the doors to creativity will open for you.

I have now become a collector of fabric. I frequently have leftovers and I've come to like them. I don't necessarily need to have a use or pending project for the fabric. I just like to have it on my shelf. It makes me feel good and sometimes it gives me inspiration. I frequently handle and touch it. It's one way I indulge myself. Leftovers are good.

I also purchase fabric because I need it. I may purchase several pieces at one time, knowing full well that the time element will prevent me from using it right away. I normally don't know what will happen to the fabric at the time I purchase it. I may have an idea, but I usually change my mind a few times before the project is complete. I encourage you to be sure to purchase enough. If you're not sure what enough is, enough is a little more than you think you need. Of course, working with more expensive fabric does require responsible consideration. It's okay to collect fabrics over a period of time before deciding what project to use them in. After all, this is a fabric collection.

Fabrics crinkle differently according to width and type. Use the chart below as a guide. There are no hard and fast rules, these are simply guidelines. Make other judgment after referring to the pattern shapes to be certain the pattern pieces will fit on the new width of crinkled fabric.

45″ cotton crinkles to 30″
60″ denim crinkles to 40″
45″ handkerchief linen crinkles to 27″
45″ sueded rayon crinkles to 30″ or slightly less
60″ wool or rayon challis crinkles to 36″
45″ lightweight Ultrasuede crinkles to 42″

When in doubt, always plan to make more crinkled fabric than needed. Any leftovers can be used for a matching handbag, belt, or the start of another garment.

How to Crinkle

The first step in crinkling is to wet the fabric. The easiest way to wet the fabric and remove excess sizing or dye is to use the washing machine, letting the machine eliminate as much excess water as possible. When a washing machine is not available, simply wet the fabric in a sink and wring out as much water as possible by hand. The hand method requires more drying time than the machine method. Ideally, I prefer to let the machine do the work for me whenever possible.

To form wrinkles, hold the selvage of one side in both hands. Work from selvage to selvage across the width or crossgrain of the fabric. The end result is vertical wrinkles going the lengthwise grain of the fabric. These are the most flattering lines for anyone, much like vertical stripes.

It's easy to gather and twist a small piece of fabric by yourself. If you are working with fabric one yard or larger, find a friend or husband who can help. It can be a bonding experience.

Gather the full width of the fabric, making small pleats and tucks with your fingers and drawing the fabric up into your hands.

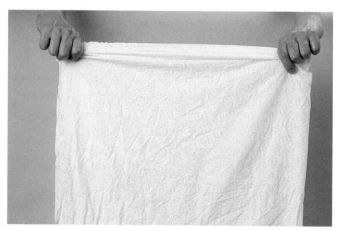

When the full width is drawn from selvage to selvage, start twisting until the fabric starts to roll on top of itself.

Lightweight fabrics form a smaller twist with more pleats. Heavier fabrics are bulkier and may not gather as easily.

Use several heavy rubber bands to hold the fabric tight as it dries. It is possible that one rubber band could break in the drying process and cause all the wrinkles and pleats to fall out. The more rubber bands used, the more interesting the wrinkles in the finished crinkled fabric.

The photo below shows three 45″-wide fabrics twisted and secured with rubber bands. The pale blue one is handkerchief linen, while the figured pieces are cotton.

Drying the Fabric

Air drying the twisted fabric may take two or three days, depending on the amount of moisture remaining in the fabric. The quickest way to dry the fabric is in the clothes dryer. Add a dry bath towel to absorb some of the moisture, aid in tumbling, and muffle the noise. Run the dryer on high for the full length of time, usually about 1½ hours. Allow the fabric to sit for a while so the moisture in the center has the opportunity to wick its way to the outside. Then run the fabric through the dryer again. The drying time will vary, depending on the amount and weight of the fabric in the bundle.

Avoid drying the fabric in one continuous timing. The constant drying will cause over-drying on the outside layer, perhaps pounding holes in the fabric, while the inside layer stays damp. Ideally, dry the fabric for an hour or so in the clothes dryer, then let it sit overnight and finish drying on the next day.

Since starting to crinkle fabric many years ago, I have met several people who like to use the microwave or oven to crinkle. I have also heard many horror stories of accidents including burning the fabric and even the house. I highly recommend using the clothes dryer or allowing the fabric to dry in open air.

When the fabric is completely dry, remove the rubber bands and open it to see the wonderful pleats, tucks, and gathers that have formed.

Isn't it amazing how we change our attitude towards wrinkles? We used to say, "I don't like that fabric because it wrinkles." Now we say, "Look at the wonderful wrinkles!"

Spread the wrinkled fabric on an ironing surface, right side down.

Don't stretch the fabric too much or the wrinkles will disappear. Refer to the chart on page 21 as a guide. Remember, fabrics will vary in the amount of wrinkles that occur because of both fabric weight and how they are handled. You may want more or fewer wrinkles than I suggest. Experiment until you find the look you like. The wrinkles are not permanent at this point. It is always possible to wet the fabric and start over before proceeding with the next step.

Setting the Wrinkles

To hold wrinkles permanently to create crinkled fabric, interface on the wrong side with a lightweight fusible interfacing. My favorite is a 60″-wide tricot (knit) type fusible interfacing. It is soft and drapes well. Because it is wide, there is no need to piece the interfacing which would cause straight line folds in the middle of wonderful wrinkles.

Woven or non-woven interfacing is generally too heavy. The crinkled fabric becomes stiff or cardboard like. If the crinkled fabric is to be used in a garment, it must drape nicely over the body. On the other hand, if the crinkled fabric is to be used for a wall hanging or on home decoration or accessories, perhaps a heavier interfacing would be preferable. Make a decision on the weight of interfacing according to the end use. Remember, the interfacing must be fusible to bond to the wrinkled fabric.

Lay the wrong side of the interfacing (the pebbled side) on the wrong side of the wrinkled fabric.

Refer to the manufacturer's instructions on the end of the bolt for proper fusing. Using plenty of steam and the wool setting on the iron, press the interfacing to the wrinkled fabric. Using an up-and-down motion, press in the direction of the pleats. Don't push the iron across the pleats or the fabric may shift.

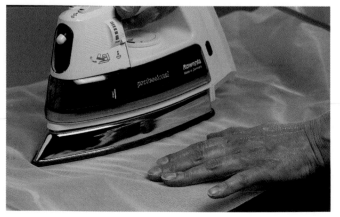

Troubleshooting

Always interface the full wrinkled fabric once it is opened. Even natural fiber fabrics are sometimes treated to avoid wrinkles. On these, if the freshly wrinkled fabric is open very long before the interfacing is applied, there is a possibility that the humidity in the air will cause the wrinkles to fall out.

Occasionally the wrong side or pebbled side of the interfacing is placed up. When the iron touches these fusing pebbles, it causes a terrific mess on the bottom of the iron. Freshly applied fusing on an iron can be removed with fabric softener dryer sheets. These sheets of pressed fibers, once used in the dryer, become great cleaning cloths for the iron. They will not scratch the iron or cause additional residue buildup. If the iron has become brown with multiple layers of fusing and starch buildup, it will be necessary to use a commercial iron cleaning product. Keep the iron as clean as possible to avoid future accidents.

Another problem that frequently happens with fusibles is that the bonding agent gets on the right side of the fabric, normally on a visible portion of the garment. Denatured alcohol will remove these little pebbles. Saturate a cotton swab with alcohol and wipe it over the stained portion. Sometimes it is necessary to use your fingernail to scrape and loosen the pebbles. After it is loosened and dried, brush away any residue with your hand. If there is interfacing on the wrong side of the fabric where the alcohol is applied, the fusing on the interfacing will loosen from the fabric. Allow the alcohol to evaporate before re-fusing the fabric to the interfacing. If the alcohol has not evaporated, the interfacing will never bond. Always test the alcohol on a corner of the fabric before using it to be certain there is no color change.

A Variety of Crinkled Fabrics

After the interfacing is fused, the crinkling process is complete. Take a look at the wonderful texture and effect you have created by simply manipulating fabric. Each fabric takes on a look of its own, from handkerchief linen to sueded rayon, cotton, rayon velvet, or wool challis.

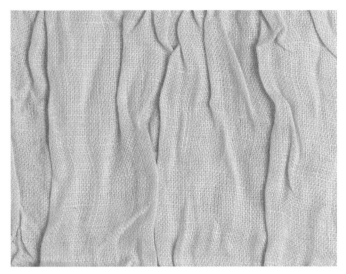

Handkerchief linen

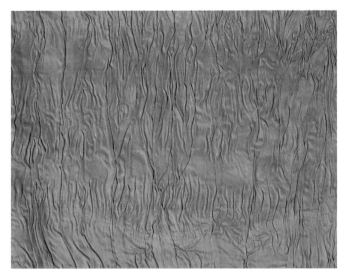

Sueded rayon

Cotton

Wool challis

In experimenting with fabric, the possibilities are unlimited and the end products are always unique. I've never destroyed a piece of fabric, although some pieces look better than others. I've discovered that some fabrics look better crinkled than they did in the first place! Study your fabric collection. Crinkle fabrics that are otherwise unappealing. It's better to crinkle a fabric than to leave it in the closet. A new challenge begins when the fabric takes on a new dimension. Lighten up, experiment, and enjoy the adventure. Besides, you have already paid for the fabric.

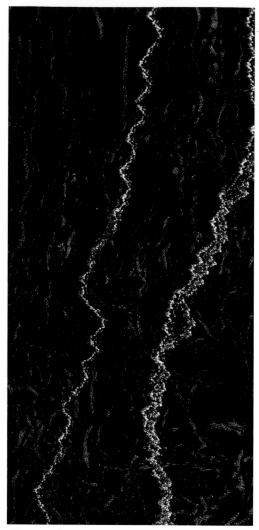
Rayon velvet

POINT OF INTEREST

↜Avoid using fabric with any polyester content for crinkling.

↜Allow a fabric length for each garment piece of crinkled fabric.

↜The washing machine will remove more moisture in the spinning cycle than hand twisting the fabric.

↜Gather the fabric for crinkling from selvage to selvage so the final wrinkles run lengthwise along the grain of the fabric.

↜Twisted fabric should be dry throughout before opening the wrinkles for interfacing.

↜Use fabric softener dryer sheets to clean fresh interfacing residue buildup from the iron.

Chapter 5

Dyeing and Bleaching Fabric

Dyeing Fabric: Impregnate with Color, Stain, Tint

My version of dyeing fabric back in the '60s was tie-dyeing. That was fun and the younger generation needs to give it a try. However, moving into the '90s and on to the new millennium, I wanted to dye fabric without big tubs, masks, and lots of mess. Upon discovering the Tumble Dye™, my dyeing techniques changed forever. The Tumble Dye pigments are the same non-toxic, water-based dyes used in the

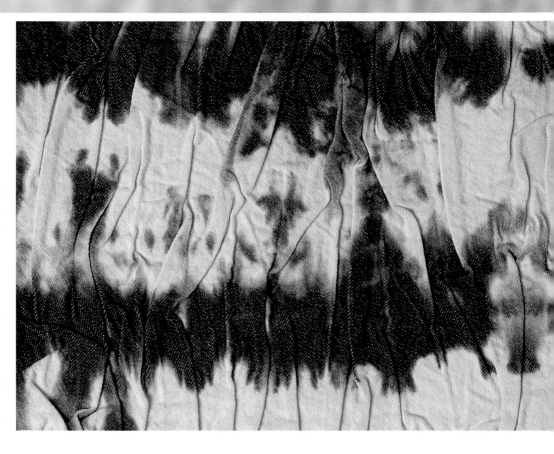

ready-to-wear industry. The dyes come in a spray bottle and the color can simply be misted on the fabric. Tumble Dye is colorfast after the fabric has been prewashed and heat set with an iron on the wool setting. There is no mixing unless you want to mix colors. And there need not be a great mess, unless you want to make one. All you have to do is cover the dyeing surface with plastic to prevent spills from permanently staining the surface. Dress accordingly and wear plastic gloves if you feel the need to protect your manicure.

The Fabric

The fabric base could be muslin or the bleached portion of a denim. My favorite is the white-on-white fabric found in great quantities at most quilt stores. A floral, leaf, swirl, or geometric design is placed on a bleached (white) or unbleached (off-white) base. As this fabric is dyed, the fabric absorbs dye differently than the design on the fabric, creating a two-tone effect. There is no great artistic ability needed to dye. The fabric does that for you.

Ribbons and Trims

Many times I find wonderful heirloom laces and embroideries in white, ecru, or champagne. When the appropriate color is not available, consider dyeing these trims to finish the look of a design. Most of these are 100% cotton and dye very well. I've also very successfully dyed 100% polyester ribbons.

No matter what fabric or product is dyed, wash it before dyeing to remove any sizing so it will absorb dye better. Any fabric that's been crinkled has been washed in the process and it's not necessary to wash it again.

Collecting the Equipment

Scout around the house, yard, or garage to collect unusual items that will add variety of shape and design. Leaves, flowers, sticks, stones, grass, chain fence, jar lids, oatmeal container lids, cardboard shapes that come in the mail or packages, cord...the list goes on and on. These things can be laid on top of the fabric. When the fabric is sprayed with dye, the shape remains protected from the dye much like a stencil effect. It's that simple.

Begin the Dyeing Process

Dyeing is another adventure with surprising results. The dyeing procedures determine the outcome. Fabric can be wet, damp, or dry. Experiment on small pieces of fabric to get the feel of the dyes.

Wet Fabric

When using wet fabric, the dyes tend to run or bleed once sprayed. Several different colors of dye sprayed simultaneously will drift or blend into each other. It is possible to maintain separate colors to a degree, but the amount of moisture in the fabric determines the amount of color concentration. Wet fabric generally results in a mellow blend of color. Pinning the fabric to a clothesline or other horizontal stand, such as a fence, will cause vertical run lines. The wind may cause the fabric to flap against the fence, resulting in very interesting formations. More streaking lines form as more dye or water is sprayed. It's an adventure.

Damp Fabric

Deeper blended shades form with damp fabric. The dyes do not run as much as on wet fabric. Use the fabric straight from the washing machine spin cycle. This is the perfect dampness for dyeing.

Dry Fabric

Splotchy tones form on dry fabric. The outcome could be misty when light touches are sprayed. Achieve a concentration of color with more saturation of dye. To avoid a concentrated circle of color, keep the bottle in constant motion while spraying from the bottle.

Fabric may be dyed flat, crinkled, or wadded in a heap. Use no particular rationale, just experiment and one thing will lead to another. Get started and things happen. Just looking at the fabric doesn't help create. No matter what the base looks like, there is another layer of threads and embellishment to be added, so any imperfections can be covered later.

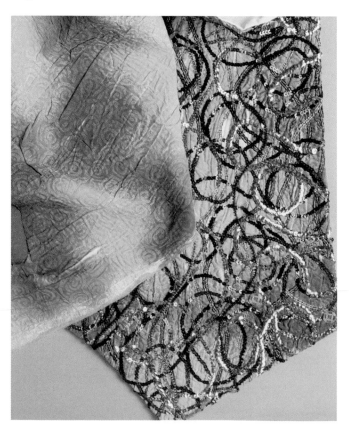

Wadding the Fabric

One of the easiest forms of dyeing with great results is to pile up the fabric in a ball. Spray the visible fabric. Because the fabric is dry, the dye does not run. At first you may feel like too much dye is concentrated in one area.

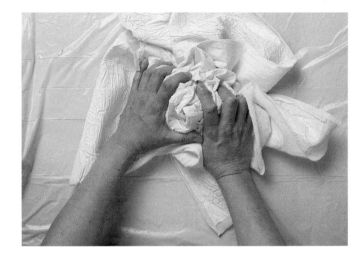

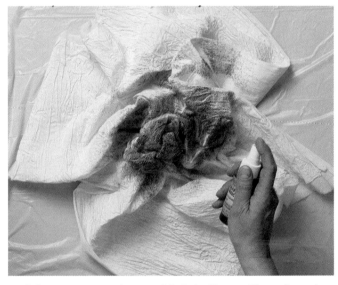

After opening the wadded ball, you'll realize that only small portions of the fabric have actually been dyed.

Wad the fabric again, pulling mostly white sections into your fingers.

To avoid overlapping colors, cover the colored section with paper.

Reopen the fabric to show your new artistic abilities.

Use the pump stem in the spray bottle as a dipper. Dip and sling. Dip and fling. This could get messy with certain age groups! It's most adventuresome.

To blend and migrate colors, mist with water after dyeing. Squeeze and bunch the fabric, causing the colors to blend together. All sorts of designs form, depending on how much the bundle is squeezed and how much water is in the fabric. Use two or three colors for the best effect.

Easy Stripes with Dyeing

The most flattering lines are diagonal. To make diagonal stripes, fold the fabric in an accordion pleat formation, allowing the folds to remain exposed.

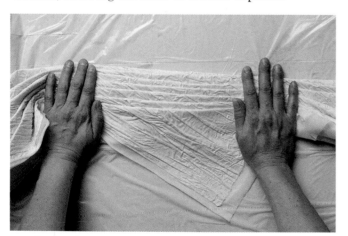

Use something heavy—pliers or a piece of wood—to hold the ends down and prevent them from unfolding. Lay strips of paper or cardboard on the last stripe to avoid over-dyeing the last stripe. Dye will not seep through the paper and color the fabric underneath.

Open the fabric to expose wonderful stripes.

To create a diamond effect, fold the fabric from opposite corners, using a desirable angle and repeat the same process. There is no need for one process to dry before adding other color. Simply continue dyeing until you get the look you want.

To add contrast to these straight diagonal lines, fling more color to create splotches.

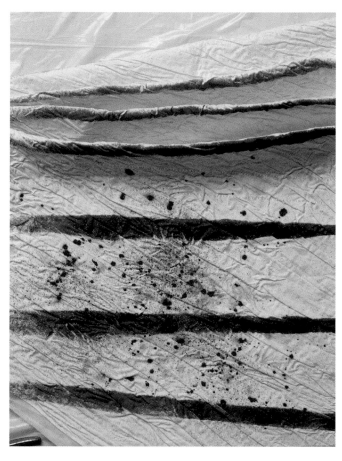

Add a little water to the bottle to avoid wasting the dye when it gets to the bottom and gently throw the dye towards the fabric. When the dye is diluted, it will migrate or spread more.

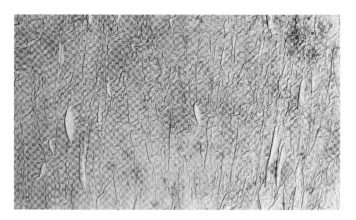

As you begin to follow these guidelines, you will lose some of your inhibitions and discover simple things you can do to create new looks. Whatever you do,

when you discover something new, remember to write it down so you will have a reference later. It's like a recipe. If you don't write it down, you'll surely forget it. Keep samples in a notebook as a guide for direction in another project. It's amazing how the creative juices start flowing once you get started.

Dyeing Embroidery Trims and Ribbon

To dye embroidery trims or ribbons, place them in a plastic bag. Mist them with water to dampen so that the dye will blend easily. Spray dye into the plastic bag. Rub the bag with your hands to evenly spread the dye throughout the trim. It may be necessary to add more dye. This is a very easy way to create a trim in the color you like.

Now that you've played with dyes for a while, the cleanup is simple. Just wash with soap and water. You will not be permanently stained.

Heat Setting

The instructions from the manufacturer suggests air drying the fabric before drying in a hot clothes dryer for 20 minutes. Always be certain the fabric is dry before using the dryer to prevent staining the inside of the dryer.

Since I normally don't have access to a clothes dryer during classes, I try to air dry the fabric on a bush, rail, or something outside in the open air while I'm demonstrating couching opportunities. In some areas of the country, in some hotels and classrooms, this works great. On rainy days and in high humidity areas, we improvise.

It's better for the fabric to dry as much as possible before heat setting with an iron. This avoids pressing the dye out of the fabric onto the ironing surface. Ideally, I like to dye the fabric, allow it to dry, and heat set by pressing all surfaces with an iron on the wool setting. Use this cooler temperature setting because of its compatibility with interfacing on crinkled fabric.

Washing Instructions

After the fabric is dyed, heat set, and embellished, wash it separately the first time to remove saturated dye. Be certain that any threads, yarns, trims, and embellishments used on the garment are washable. Always use non-chlorinated detergent.

It's true that most of your dyeing will be further embellished. These garments will probably be washed occasionally rather than frequently. Use cool water, wash separately on gentle, and line dry. I've been very successful with this method of cleaning my garments. Be aware that some dry cleaners do not want to bother with embellished garments. If they don't want to take a risk, don't push them.

POINT OF INTEREST

- ALWAYS PRE-WASH FABRIC TO REMOVE SIZING BEFORE DYEING.
- TO AVOID ROUND SPLOTCHES OF COLOR, KEEP THE BOTTLE IN CONSTANT MOTION WHEN SPRAYING, AIMING TOWARDS THE FABRIC AND NOT THE WALL OR FLOOR.
- BE CERTAIN THE FABRIC IS ON THE TABLE BEFORE DYEING. ANY OVERLAP OVER THE EDGE OF THE TABLE WILL RESULT IN A STRAIGHT LINE.
- DYE RIBBONS AND TRIMS IN A PLASTIC BAG.
- HEAT SET DYED FABRIC USING AN IRON ON THE WOOL SETTING OR IN A HOT CLOTHES DRYER FOR 20 MINUTES.
- ALWAYS DRY FABRIC BEFORE ATTEMPTING TO STITCH. IT IS NEVER A GOOD IDEA TO STITCH ON DAMP FABRIC.
- DON'T BE AFRAID TO EXPERIMENT AND TRY NEW IDEAS THAT ARISE ONCE YOU GET STARTED. DYEING IS TERRIFIC FUN.

Bleaching:
To Whiten or Fade

Traditionally, bleach is used to brighten white fabric, remove stains, disinfect, and deodorize. Some colored fabrics can be safely bleached. Though color removers may be the most practical choice for removing color in fabric, bleaching is an option. I am particularly intrigued with bleaching cotton denim.

Whenever experimenting, I like to do the worst thing I feel my students could ever do. So one day while crinkling denim, I decided to bleach it. The fabric was dampened, twisted tightly, and held with several rubber bands. The wad of fabric was placed in an empty washing machine so any splashes would not spread to other objects or fabric. Bleach was poured directly from the bottle onto the twisted fabric ball. Some bleach ran off the fabric into the washing machine tub. Other bleach stopped in some of the wrinkles and twists, forming a puddle. It eventually absorbed into the denim. During the pouring process, bleach had touched every visible portion of the denim fabric—the idea being to completely whiten some area of the denim and combine color with white or pastel shades in other areas.

Bleach remained on this particular piece of denim for about 1½ hours before I filled the machine with water and ran the complete wash and rinse cycle twice. The denim remained twisted with rubber bands throughout the whole process of bleaching, rinsing, and drying. This enabled the final wrinkles to correspond with the whitened areas.

Bleaching times may vary, depending on the fabric. On future denim bleaching projects, I discovered that the bleach may discolor the fabric instantly or it may take a while. Not knowing what dyes were used in the construction of the fabric, be prepared to wash the fabric immediately or allow the bleach to stand for some time. Never leave bleach on a fabric any longer than 1½ hours because the fabric will begin to deteriorate and holes will form. Of course, this could be the added texture you desire.

POINT OF INTEREST

☞ ALWAYS BLEACH FABRIC IN A WELL VENTILATED ROOM. NEVER MIX BLEACH WITH OTHER HOUSEHOLD CHEMICALS OR LIQUIDS. HAZARDOUS GASES COULD FORM. ONCE THE BLEACH IS RINSED FROM THE FABRIC, THERE WILL BE NO FURTHER DISCOLORATION OR DETERIORATION OF THE FABRIC.

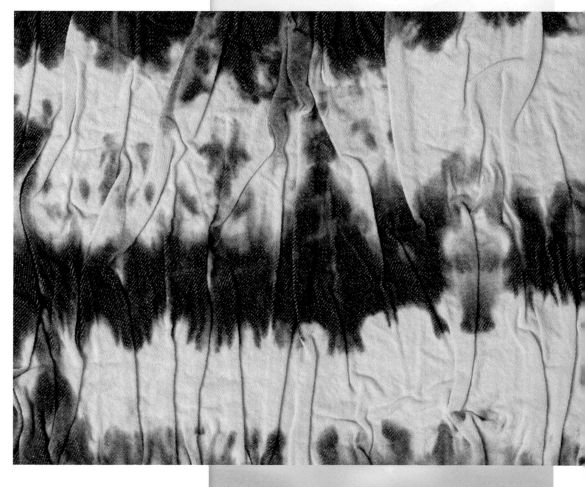

Chapter 6

Decorative Stitching

DECORATIVE STITCHING: THE USE OF DECORATIVE THREADS OF DIFFERENT COLOR, TEXTURE, AND FIBER IN VARIOUS STITCHES TO CREATE ATTRACTIVE, STRIKING, OR FESTIVE DETAILS.

Decorative stitching is accomplished using the varied stitches built into a sewing machine. It also can be executed by changing the appearance of a basic machine stitch with length and width alterations.

Most machines have a variety of stitches that would look wonderful on crinkled or flat fabric.

There are many stitches common to every brand of machine, even when only a few stitches are built in. Although a machine may have a built-in setting for a stitch, it is easy to change the width and/or length for a completely different look. Always consider this option no matter what stitch you use.

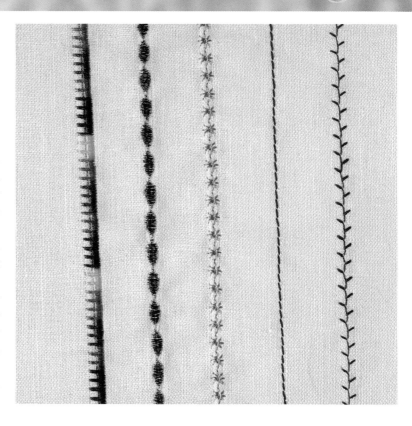

Type of Thread	Type of Needle	Stitch
rayon	embroidery	decorative & straight
metallic	metallica	decorative & straight
lamé	metallica	decorative & straight
acrylic	embroidery	decorative & straight
silk	embroidery	decorative & straight
topstitching/buttonhole twist, jeans	topstitch	best with longer & open decorative stitches; avoid satin decorative stitches
variegated	according to thread type	shows off color gradation best with decorative satin stitches; subtle in straight stitches; great with open decorative stitches
two threads of same type in one needle	topstitch	straight stitch for bolder appearance; slightly open satin stitches; works with most threads except topstitching

Threads

There is an enormous variety of thread available on the market today. Some of my very favorite threads are variegated, though I do use many solid color decorative threads. I believe these threads are sometimes overlooked because of their appearance on the spool.

Add a few of them to your sewing collection. You will be pleased with the outcome on decorative, more open stitches, as well as relatively straight stitches.

I've come to the conclusion that threads can be classified in two basic categories. A thread that's small enough to go through the eye of a sewing machine needle and will stitch without breaking can be referred to as a needle thread. A thread too large to go through a sewing machine needle will be couched and is referred to as a couching thread.

The selection of thread types has changed drastically in the past few years. It's wonderful to see the variety of threads that can be used in the sewing machine needle. Some threads are larger or more fragile, making the needle size and type a very important consideration. Generally, when problems arise, proper threading of the machine or needle type are the first things to check. Most times, the thread tension should be loosened slightly to accommodate these more fragile threads.

When constantly changing from one thread type to another on a project, I sometimes use the top-stitching needle to avoid changing needles so frequently. This works for me, particularly on crinkled fabric. Always test on a scrap of fabric from the project to be certain you like the look of the stitch. Sometimes a too-large needle will cause holes where the needle penetrates, so testing is a must.

Bobbin Thread

It's possible to stitch many layers of decorative stitching on one project, causing a buildup of thread that can make a garment very stiff or cardboard like. To maintain a soft draping fabric, it's best to use a bobbin thread designed for the purpose. Every thread company on the market that designs thread for embroidery has a bobbin thread. I prefer 100% cotton 60 or 70 weight thread. It's very lightweight, preventing the multiple layers of stitching from becoming bulky. This thread is not intended for garment construction. Other bobbin threads available are lingerie, nylon, and polyester. Choose the one that works best with your machine. It never hurts to test and keep track of your preferences.

Always fill several bobbins at once before beginning to stitch. It's amazing how much thread some decorative stitches use. When the bobbin runs out, simply remove it and replace it with a full bobbin. There will be no skipped stitches and the pattern will continue as though the thread were endless.

The Straight Stitch

Don't feel obligated to begin with a decorative stitch. A heavier thread, such as buttonhole twist, topstitching, or jeans thread, works beautifully with a straight stitch. The stitched lines could be crooked or straight. No matter which you choose to do—meander around the fabric or sew very straight parallel lines—it is best to use longer stitches. The topstitching needle will make this an easy embellishment. Use a variety of colors for variety.

Evelyn Dix

Beginning to Stitch

There are so many stitches on new sewing machines, but the fun begins when the playing starts. With a few new approaches or a little incentive, even utility stitches become embellishment. It's so much fun to change the rules and make something different.

Set up the machine with a decorative thread of your choice, the proper needle, and a full bobbin. Choose a stitch, preferably one you've never used before, and begin stitching. Change the stitch width and length just for the fun of it. When I find a new appearance for one of my programmed stitches, I record the settings in my machine instruction manual or notebook. This avoids the problem of depending on memory. Another helpful aid is a log of different fabric, thread, and stitch combinations for future reference.

Zigzag for Variety

The zigzag is the most versatile stitch on a sewing machine. Used as an open stitch, it has many different width options. The stitch length can be shortened to form a satin stitch for appliqué and embroidery techniques.

For a completely different appearance, set the machine for a perfect satin stitch (a length adjustment). Begin on a narrow width and gradually increase to the widest stitch as the machine feeds the fabric. Then, continuing with the stitching, do the reverse until the machine reduces the width to zero. Move the fabric in a curve as you sew. Don't pull the fabric or an open stitch will form. Simply guide the fabric in different directions as the machine feeds, changing the stitch width as you go. The effect can be as varied as your whim.

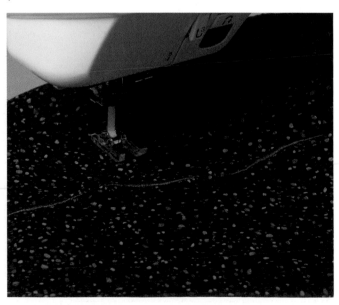

Irregular Satin Stitching

Take a look at the irregular satin zigzag stitch. Change the stitch width and length slightly rather than conforming to the machine settings. The width is wider and the length is shorter.

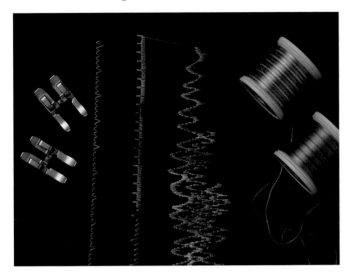

Using two decorative threads in a topstitching needle fills in the stitch to make it fuller. The open toe embroidery foot allows the layers of stitching to pass under the foot more easily. Some variegated threads, particularly those that don't match in color variety, are considerably different when sewn through the same needle. Or choose a variegated thread in combination with a solid color thread. Change the stitch width and length slightly rather than conforming to the machine settings. Meander over the fabric, whether flat or crinkled, giving the fabric a slight tug from side-to-side while the machine is in motion. A delicate pull will not strain the needle or machine in any way.

After completing the first row of stitching, add another row close or almost parallel to the first. Occasionally overlap the stitches and other times let all the fabric peek through, forming a braid appearance. Several rows may be stitched in this manner for a wider braid. Consider making several rows of braiding illusion in varying widths.

The Double Needle

Using the same two spools of thread and the same stitch, switch to a 1.6 double needle. As stitching progresses, the threads will lay side-by-side rather than overlap.

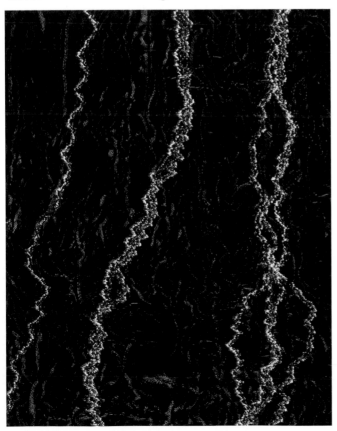

The double needle keeps the threads separated to differentiate the separate colors, while the single needle overlaps the thread in a single stitch.

A completely different color may appear. Combining threads is similar to combining dyes. They take on a completely different coloring when stitched through one needle or a double needle.

Test or hand walk the machine through the stitch to be sure the double needle clears the presser foot. Most machines have buttons to press when working with a double needle. These buttons prevent the machine from stitching so wide that the needle touches the presser foot. On most machines, this button was designed to use with the pintucking feet. The needle hole may be smaller on this foot than the open toe embroidery foot. Rather than push the button, hand walk the machine through the stitch to be certain the needle clears the foot to avoid breaking any needles.

The Fringe Foot

The fringe foot was designed originally to make tailor tacks. It's more versatile and decorative as a fringe foot.

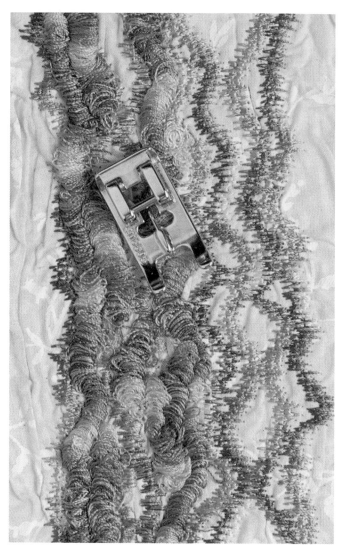

Place two threads through the topstitching needle for fuller fringe. Set the machine for narrow to medium zigzag to clear the bar on the foot. Loosen the tension to almost zero. The object is for the decorative thread to form loops on the top and the bobbin thread to remain unseen. As the needle stitches over the bar in the foot, extra loops or fringe are formed. Before beginning, tie off the threads by stitching in position. When a row of stitching is complete, tie off the threads and lift the presser foot. Pull the last few stitches from the bar area off the foot.

Fill in blank areas of fabric with this dimensional stitch. Some rows may be stitched the full length of the project like the seaweed.

Madra Prater

Other times a small area of fringing is more suitable.

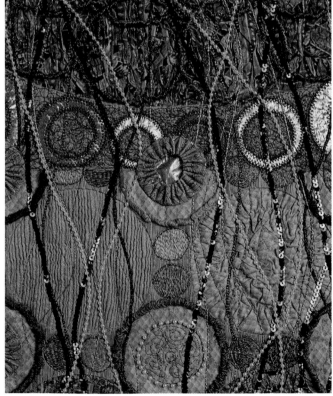

Madra Prater

The fringe was perfect for eyelashes.

Judy Kriehn

The collection of threads may change throughout a project. Don't feel obligated to stay with the same color thread or the same type of thread. Combinations of blending and contrast create entirely different looks. The options are endless. Enjoy the fun of creating new texture.

POINT OF INTEREST

↝WHEN CONSTANTLY CHANGING FROM ONE THREAD TYPE TO ANOTHER, I SOMETIMES USE THE TOPSTITCHING NEEDLE TO AVOID CHANGING NEEDLES SO FREQUENTLY.

↝ALWAYS FILL SEVERAL BOBBINS AT ONCE WHEN PREPARING TO DECORATIVE STITCH. WHEN ONE EMPTIES, REPLACE IT WITH A FULL BOBBIN.

↝KEEP BOBBIN THREAD BOBBINS SEPARATE FROM ALL-PURPOSE THREADS TO AVOID CONSTRUCTING A GARMENT WITH BOBBIN THREAD.

↝ALWAYS TEST BEFORE STITCHING ON A PROJECT. THREAD COLORS MAY CHANGE, THE TENSION MAY BE TOO TIGHT OR LOOSE, OR YOU MAY NOT LIKE THE STITCH ON THAT PRINT.

↝ ALWAYS USE LAMÉ THREADS ON A VERTICAL SPOOL HOLDER TO AVOID TWISTING, STRETCHING, AND BREAKING THE THREAD. FOR MACHINES WITH HORIZONTAL SPOOL HOLDERS, THERE IS AN ADAPTER TO SUBSTITUTE.

Chapter 7

Couching

By definition, couching is a method of embroidery where a design is created by hand or machine stitching over threads, cords, or yarns that have been arranged on the surface of a material. With the availability of more embellishments such as sequins, beads, pearls, and ribbons, and additional feet introduced by machine companies, couching is taking on a new dimension.

The market is overflowing with wonderful threads designed for the upper and lower loopers on sergers, yet heavy enough to use in the sewing machine needle. These metallic threads, braids, ombres and ribbons, pearl rayons and cottons, and other decorative yarns are perfect for couching.

Other threads and yarns intended for hand embroidery, needlepoint, knitting, and related crafts can transfer to couching. They glide through the foot, maintaining their position and making couching by machine a simple, quick process for creating an ornament or trim.

Needle and Needle Thread

Review the needle threads, needles, and bobbin thread suggested in the Decorative Stitching chapter. These guidelines apply to couching. The difference is that needle threads are used to secure heavier threads, ribbons, and embellishments. These heavier threads will be referred to as couching threads to avoid confusion with needle threads.

Planning the Layers

Each type of couching thread and ribbon could have multiple options for couching. To begin, apply the widest, flattest layers first, in colors that need to be subtle in the project. As layers progress, add the more bulky layers like edgestitched ribbon, beads, and sequin yardage.

1/4″ Satin Ribbon

When a centered stitching is desired on 1/4″ ribbon, use the open toe embroidery foot. The ribbon fits perfectly between the toes of the foot, making accuracy a breeze. More open decorative stitches, staggered satin stitches, the honeycomb stitch, or double needle feather stitches produce a beautiful texture. Experiment with the stitch length and width for different effects. Be careful with the stitch width when using the double needle. The wider the distance between the needles, the narrower the width must be to prevent the needle from breaking. The double needle button on most new machines allows the machine to stitch up to a certain width. Be sure to push the button.

Ribbon Thread and 1/8″ Ribbon

Ribbon thread or floss and 1/8″ satin ribbon are suitable for couching in a variety of ways. Use the braiding foot to center the ribbon by the needle. Set the decorative stitch width to allow the needle to go over the edge of the ribbon and not beyond. Consider the daisy, ladder, or feather stitch for these narrow ribbons or any stitch with open spaces for the ribbon to show. Combinations of stitches are another alternative using memory.

Ribbon thread is a bias thread. Spread the end and pull one of the fibers.

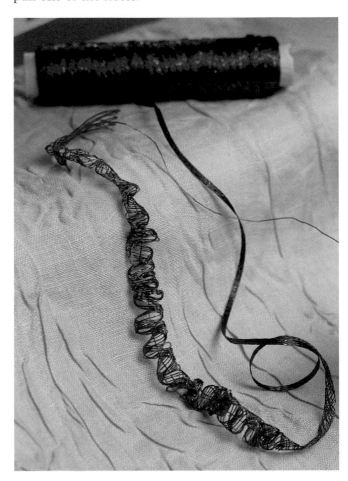

For a final layer in the project, this ruched thread makes an elegant texture. Use the open toe embroidery foot to apply the gathered ribbon, being careful to avoid catching the loops on the foot. Use an open decorative stitch to apply. Cut the pulled thread after the stitching is complete.

Serger Threads

Heavier threads for the serger loopers are easy to couch single or twisted with other colors.

The tendency is to match colors so well that they are not visible once stitched. Add a contrast in color for

visibility. Use thread colors you would never buy in fabric. Thread is only a small portion of the garment. Notice the sparkle the lime green adds to the twisted purple, blue, and pink.

The Proper Stitch

Most instructions I have seen suggest using a zigzag stitch to hold these twisted threads in position. That mats the beautiful threads down. My preference is the multi-step zigzag stitch. Alter the stitch width to the width of the twisted threads. Lengthen the stitch to about 1.5 or 2. Though using variegated thread that does not match, the needle thread is barely visible. It doesn't draw attention to itself, but adds sparkle to the couching thread.

Occasionally I work with braids or ribbons that are so tightly woven it's difficult for the needle to penetrate using the multi-step zigzag stitch. In this case, use a clear monofilament thread in the needle and a zigzag stitch. Be sure the needle swings over these couching threads rather than piercing them to avoid pulls.

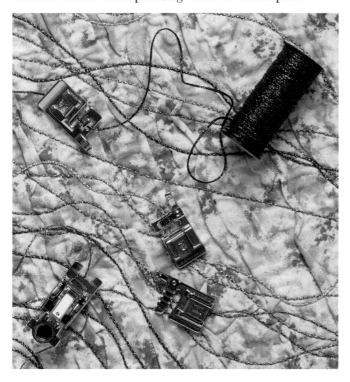

Choose the foot with the hole closest to the size of the couching threads to maintain proper alignment. A too-large hole will cause the couching threads to move around too much, missing stitches. A too-small hole will catch on the couching threads, causing the fabric to gather. Some feet have an adjustable screw to alter the size of the hole.

Multi-Hole Cording Foot

Cording feet with tiny holes through which three to nine heavier threads may pass allow many combinations of types and colors of thread. The different holes align the threads perfectly, resulting in the illusion of ribbon.

A subtle variegated design is achieved with slightly different shades of a color or a bolder appearance with sharper brighter colors. The possibilities are endless because a great variety of colors is available in specialty threads.

My Favorite Stitch	Width & Length Changes	Needle	Thread
_____	_____	_____	_____
_____	_____	_____	_____
_____	_____	_____	_____
_____	_____	_____	_____
_____	_____	_____	_____

Ordinarily, all holes in the foot are threaded at once. Just because there are a number of holes in a foot does not mean all holes must be used at the same time. Creativity happens when rules are broken. Sometimes only the outer holes are used with a decorative stitch set to the maximum width.

Other times odd holes are used, allowing space between the lines of couching threads. Incorporate a variety of uses from the same foot into the same project. Every row stitched can be a different application.

Twisted Threads

To create a dimensional corded appearance with yarn, use the open toe embroidery foot and a straight stitch. Find the center of a long yarn and secure it to the fabric by backstitching. Lift the pressure and pull the yarn on top of the foot, holding the yarn away from the needle.

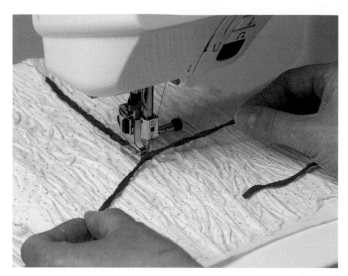

Use the needle down position. Stitch three or four straight stitches. Stop. Alternate the yarn from one side to the other. Continue this process in the area desired. Use your sewing machine's memory function when possible to get consistent lengths between twists or make the twists obviously different.

Another option is to use yarn of contrasting color or texture. Tack the two yarns at the beginning of a seam. Place one yarn to the right of the needle and the other yarn to the left. Establish a pattern of alternating the yarns. Always twist left over right, left over right. Or twist so the preferred yarn is always on top. Sometimes this takes a little concentration.

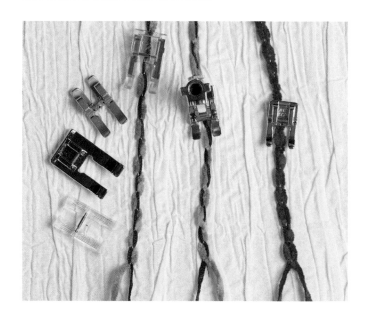

Ric Rac and Ribbon for Dimension

Twist ric rac together to form a narrow braid. Meander this new braid over the garment with clear monofilament thread and the open toe foot.

Ribbon 1/4˝ and wider is more versatile than ever. The edgestitching foot permits accurate sewing along one edge. When the ribbon is couched in wavy lines, the curves add extra dimension. Use a straight stitch or decorative stitch just over one edge of the ribbon, making the other edge move into outer space.

Two rows of ribbon may be attached at one time, much like combining laces with heirloom sewing. Both sides of the ribbon may be attached or one side left to float.

Sequins

Add a festive appearance to any wearable by adding sequin yardage. Sequins should be applied before beads, since they are flatter. It is easy to meander sequins over a project, intersecting when the design so requires.

With monofilament thread in the needle and the open toe foot, zigzag over the sequins.

Set the stitch width slightly wider than the sequin size, preventing the needle from piercing the sequin. The stitch length should be slightly shorter than the width. Because there is a nap to sequin yardage, the smooth direction should be placed so that it runs with the foot. If the sequins constantly catch on the foot, reverse the direction. They should glide through the foot without hesitation. After applying the sequins, slide your finger over the sequins, making the monofil-

ament thread move between the sequin overlap. Presto, the monofilament thread disappears.

Couching is an excellent way to get acquainted with your machine to see exactly what it can do. With each new generation of sewing machines, there are more and exciting decorative stitches and opportunities to expand your specialty sewing techniques and skills.

When I learned to sew, I was taught to make straight lines. When couching, it is more fun to create curvy or wavy lines. It's easier to design asymmetrically. Meander wherever there is a need for more stitching without consideration of straight lines. Stitch between and around the wrinkles and tucks. Fold back or open up a large tuck to add more dimension. Wander around the design in the printed fabric. Use the mirror image or combine several stitches with your machine's memory. I never dreamed years ago that I would eventually sew crooked on wrinkled fabric.

POINT OF INTEREST

↜ ALWAYS TEST NEEDLE THREAD AND COUCHING THREAD COMBINATIONS. SOMETIMES THEY CHANGE COLORS AFTER THEY'RE STITCHED.

↜ WHENEVER POSSIBLE, BEGIN AND END ON THE CUT EDGE OF THE GARMENT.

↜ COUCHING MAY CAUSE THE BASE FABRIC TO SHRINK SLIGHTLY. CUT OUT THE GARMENT 1˝ LARGER BEFORE BEGINNING TO STITCH. THIS ALLOWS FOR SHRINKAGE IN STITCHING AND AIDS WITH EMBELLISHMENT PLACEMENT.

↜ USE THE FOOT THAT MAKES THE TASK EASIER FOR LESS STRAIN ON THE EYES AND BACK.

↜ WHEN THREADING IS DIFFICULT, USE A FLOSS THREADER TO THREAD THE FOOT.

↜ EFFECTIVE COUCHING USES THREADS OF HIGH CONTRAST COLOR AND TEXTURE. THE SPOOLS OF THREAD LAYING SIDE-BY-SIDE MAY LOOK AWFUL TOGETHER. TWIST SEVERAL THREADS TOGETHER BEFORE FORMING AN OPINION. SOMETIMES WHAT LOOKS UGLY ON THE SPOOL BECOMES WONDERFUL IN SMALL AMOUNTS.

↜ NOTE ANY COMBINATIONS OF STITCHES OR DESIGNS IN A MANUAL FOR LATER REFERENCE. IT'S EASY TO FORGET.

↜ HAVE SEVERAL FULL BOBBINS HANDY. DECORATIVE STITCHES USE MORE THREAD THAN STRAIGHT STITCHES. NOTHING IS MORE AGGRAVATING THAN TO RUN OUT OF THREAD IN THE MIDDLE OF A ROW OF STITCHES. WHEN THIS HAPPENS, SIMPLY RETHREAD THE BOBBIN AND CONTINUE.

↜ TO HIDE A SKIPPED STITCH, OVERLAP ANOTHER ROW OF COUCHING. THE INTERSECTION WILL HIDE THE BROKEN LINE OF STITCHES. IT'S NOT NECESSARY TO RELOCATE THE NEEDLE INTO THE STITCH PATTERN.

↜ COUCH ON PIECED STRIPS AFTER THE SPIRAL TUBE IS OPENED. IT'S DIFFICULT TO STITCH ON VERY NARROW PIECING WITHOUT DISTORTING THE PIECING.

↜ COUCHING IS A WONDERFUL OPPORTUNITY TO BECOME CREATIVE WITH THE COLLECTION IN YOUR STOCKPILE.

Chapter 8

Beading

BEAD: A SMALL, SHAPED PIECE OF HARD MATERIAL PIERCED FOR THREADING WITH OTHERS ON A STRING OR WIRE, OR FOR SEWING ON A FABRIC.
BEADING: ORNAMENTATION WITH BEADS.

One of the best ways to add sparkle and glitz to any project is with beading. Since my expertise is in the area of machine sewing, any beads I sew with are sewn by machine. There is a variety of beading-by-the-yard available, from molded plastic to rhinestone to glass Cross-Locked™ (my favorite). These beads are interwoven with cotton thread, allowing them to be flexible and evenly spaced. They can be sewn by machine quickly with little effort.

The Piping or Beading Foot

A piping foot with a zigzag hole allows the beading to pass through the groove under the foot. The foot guides the beading to avoid the problem of breaking needles or beads.

It's tempting to mark lines directly on the fabric for beading placement, but it's easier to guide the beading

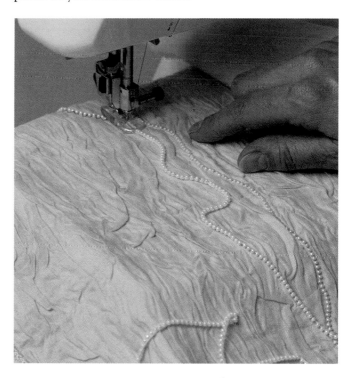

as you sew, curving the foot around the tucks and pleats as you encounter them.

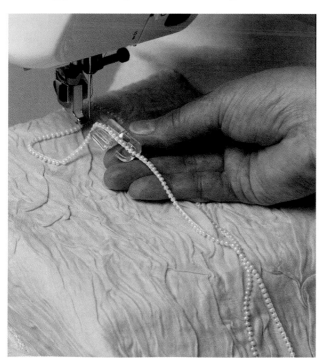

Needle and Thread

Use the needle that corresponds to the weight of the fabric. Usually an 80/12 needle with monofilament thread is a good starting point. Use an all-purpose cotton/poly thread in the bobbin. Begin with a full bobbin since you will use a great deal of thread.

Setting the Machine

Machine settings will vary depending on the machine brand and the bead type and size. Place beads in the groove of the foot and hand walk the machine through the stitch to be certain the needle clears the beads. The settings will probably be medium width and medium length. As you sew, the monofilament thread will slide off the bead, making the stitching virtually impossible to see.

Occasionally the bobbin thread may rise to the top. If this happens, loosen the tension slightly so the only thread visible from the top is the clear thread holding the beads in place.

There should be a stitch for every bead. If the mono-filament thread is visible to the side of the bead (almost like a spider web), the stitch is too wide. If the stitch passes two beads, the stitch is too long. If the machine needle touches the bead, the stitch is too narrow. Once the zigzag is set properly for the size beads being applied, rows of beading can be attached in a short time.

Plan to have rows begin and end in a seam allow-ance to avoid the necessity of tediously hand stitching the final bead.

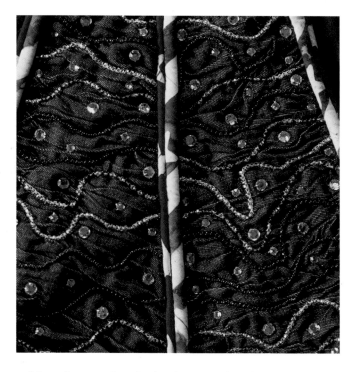

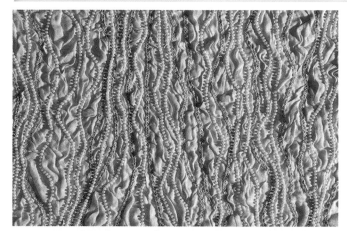

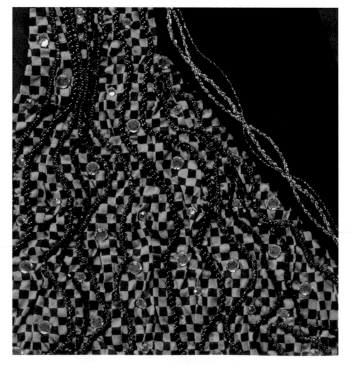

Use pliers to break the last few beads in the seam allowance to avoid extra bulk. By breaking the beads rather than pulling them from the string, the inter-locked thread will remain locked.

It's possible to crisscross beads in a project but it's very tedious. The beads will be very close together, making it difficult for the needle to stitch. The best way to accomplish crossing a row of beads over anoth-er row of beads is to hand walk the machine over the area where the beads are close together. If the needle feels like it's going to touch a bead, it's possible to stop before breaking a needle or bead. The best place to cross over another row of beads is where a bead has broken, allowing extra space for the bead intersec-tions.

Chapter 9

Appliqué

Appliqué has become one of the most recognized forms of embellishment. In appliqué, a design is applied to the surface of another fabric using hand or machine stitching, glue, or fusing. There are many varieties of this art, from somewhat intricate to fairly simple designs. When limited time is a major factor, consider the less complicated techniques as well as the most fun ones. This puts ticker tape appliqué, leaf appliqué, and traditional appliqué made easy at the top of the list.

Preparing the Garment

One of the best additions to a wardrobe is a crinkled vest with appliqué. Cut out the vest 1″ larger than the finished size. This allows some freedom for shrinkage and provides the basic size and shape of the pattern. You can easily see the position of the center front, neck edge, and armscye, which prevents you from placing a wonderful design element in a bad spot.

Appliqué Fabric

Choose the appliqué fabric for the appearance desired. Color—shiny, dull, napped, and textured—plays a part in the finished look. A small portion of a color can highlight the finished design. Do not plan to match colors exactly or you may get frustrated. It's okay to have slightly off colors in the same project. I once used tomato red, burgundy red, and blue red in the same project. There wasn't a tremendous amount of any one of the colors, just enough to draw the eye to each section. The project was wonderful. No one really noticed that the colors were such an awful combination in the garment. It worked.

Fusing Basics

To begin, place a paper-backed fusing medium on the wrong side of the fabric. Steam-A-Seam 2® will stick to fabric for a temporary hold. The bond becomes permanent only when heat is applied. This makes it most desirable for appliqué arranging and rearranging. Keep in mind that the wrong side of a fabric could easily become the right side if you so choose. It's proper to have both sides of the fabric showing in the same project. Sometimes this is just the right contrast for variety.

Ticker Tape Appliqué

Before removing the paper from the back, cut irregular shapes such as circles, triangles, stars, etc. in different sizes for the appliqué fabric. Use scissors, pinking shears, a rotary cutter, or some of the decorative wavy rotary blades to add character to the design. It's easier to cut shapes before removing the paper because there is more stability. Another option is to draw pattern designs directly on the paper. One word of caution— the design should be drawn on the paper with a mirror image when a one-way design is desired, such as letters or a sewing machine design.

After cutting the shapes, remove the paper from the appliqué. Position it on the background fabric in a decorative manner and steam it to hold it in place. Steam works best with most fusibles on the wool setting of many irons. Avoid a problem by testing with scrap fabric before going to the real project. Many irons run hotter than others or produce different amounts of steam.

The purpose of this step is simply to hold the appliqué in position for stitching. Don't over-press. Many fabrics such as lamé and synthetic suede will change appearance or melt with too much heat. This variety of appliqué is very quick. It's designed to add texture and dimension. Some of the design may ravel or fray with wear, but that's fine. Perfection with covered edges is another type of appliqué. This one is fun and relieves tension rather than adding to it.

Threads

Though any threads will work fine for ticker tape appliqué, experiment with topstitching or buttonhole twist thread. These are heavier threads that work beautifully in the topstitching needle. The eye is large enough to handle the thread without fraying or breaking.

Decorative threads like rayon or metallic can also be threaded in this needle. The eye and shank allow the bulk of the thread to glide through the machine. Simple measures such as using the proper needle with decorative threads make sewing a breeze.

Stitching

Now comes the fun part. Stitch up and down and all around with the basic foot. You may find the open toe embroidery foot offers more visibility if you choose. Overlap some of the stitches. Allow some areas to remain blank while others become covered with many stitches.

A longer straight stitch is suitable for topstitching thread or try more open decorative stitches. Remember, there are no set rules, so stitch, stitch, stitch until there is no more thread! Then grab another spool and keep going.

- THERE IS NO SET PATTERN FOR SHAPES IN TICKER TAPE APPLIQUÉ. JUST USE THE ROTARY CUTTER AND CUT THE SHAPES. SHAPES DON'T HAVE TO BE PERFECT.

- USE TICKER TAPE APPLIQUÉ AS AN OPPORTUNITY TO USE UP SMALL QUANTITIES OF THREAD LEFT ON A SPOOL.
- FEEL FREE TO SEW CROOKED WITH TICKER TAPE APPLIQUÉ.

Leaf Appliqué

The most common method of appliqué uses satin stitches (the zigzag stitch with short stitch length) around the outer edge of the fabric being applied to the base. Though this method can be fairly easy to accomplish, some patterns have many curves, corners, and points. These are the areas that require expertise and perfection and sometimes take more time than desired for a small project. It can be just as attractive, add more dimension, and be less time consuming to stitch within the pattern rather than the border of the appliqué.

Take, for instance, a simple leaf pattern. The inside and outside curves are relatively sharp, making the stitching very tedious, particularly with a wide satin stitch. Rather than stitch around the outside edge of the design, stitch only the veins with a satin stitch, allowing the outer edges to hang loose. Use a stitch width proportionate to the size of the leaf itself, usually 1½ to 2. This width is easier to turn and manipulate.

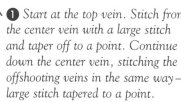

1 *Start at the top vein. Stitch from the center vein with a large stitch and taper off to a point. Continue down the center vein, stitching the offshooting veins in the same way — large stitch tapered to a point.*

16 *Stitch the center vein last, covering the large bulky stitches created in making the offshooting veins. Taper off at the end.*

Starting Point

Consider the starting point. The stem appears to be the most logical beginning, but study the veins. The tiny veins branch from a larger vein to nothing at the tip of the leaf. This could easily become the design in the appliqué, making each leaf appear alive. With stitching solely in the veins and stem, the outer edges of the leaf are loose, free, and floating just as if they are falling from a tree.

The Natural Progression

Adapt this idea to the sewing machine. By turning the stitch width knob from wide to narrow or nothing, the stitching could look similar to a natural leaf. But there are so many points extending from the same vein. Begin with a satin stitch width of 1½ to 2 in the center vein of the leaf. Sew to nothing at the point. The tiny straight stitches at the point finish the end without backstitching. The beginning is covered by the next row of stitches.

The progression of this process may appear a little odd or backwards at first but after making several leaves, the finished product is smoother, quicker, and more natural. The wider beginning stitches are concealed by the curves in the other veins. It is less complicated to sew from wide to narrow than it is from narrow to wide. Remember to keep it simple.

Synthetic suede like Ultrasuede makes wonderful appliqués because it doesn't ravel. But there is no reason a woven fabric can't be used with this same technique. Use several layers of fabric for one leaf or transfer this same idea to a flower. The layers add dimension and the ravels add texture.

Threads

Consider the variety of threads for the needle. Fine cotton embroidery thread adds sheen. Rayon and acrylic add nice shine. Metallic and lamé add glitz. Determine the desired finished appearance and choose the needle thread accordingly. Typically the best needle is the embroidery or Metallica needle to avoid thread breaking problems.

Bobbin Thread: Because so much thread is used in appliqué, fill the bobbin with bobbin thread or cotton embroidery thread. It's finer thread, allowing the bobbin to hold more with fewer bobbin changes. If an extra bobbin is handy, the empty one can be replaced quickly without cutting the needle thread. Stitching continues with a nice even flow. There is no starting and stopping to fill bobbins, just changing to a full bobbin when one is empty.

Open Toe Foot

The process of appliqué requires a special sewing foot. The front area of the open toe appliqué foot permits the stitcher to view every corner, curve, and point as they appear, improving precision stitching. The bottom of the foot contains a small flat groove, permitting the stitching to flow to the back of the foot without buildup or bulk. The proper foot makes the application easier. Take pleasure in creating a new version of appliqué.

- ☛ USE THE SEWING MACHINE NEEDLE THAT CORRESPONDS TO THE TYPE OF THREAD USED.
- ☛ USE FINE BOBBIN THREAD TO AVOID BULKY STITCHES.
- ☛ FILL SEVERAL BOBBINS AT ONCE TO AVOID HAVING TO FILL THEM IN THE MIDDLE OF A STITCHING PATTERN.

POINT OF INTEREST

Traditional Appliqué Made Easy

There are many appliqué patterns on the market, but you may also consider using the design in the fabric itself as a pattern. Choose a basic design.

Eliminate some of the fine lines in the design. Make an enlarged copy of the fabric on a copy machine. This is a simple way to produce an appliqué pattern. If you are artistic, feel free to draw designs. However, if you have limited time and prefer the appliqué to be an exact enlargement, use a copy machine. Aside from saving time, this will allow you the freedom to manipulate pattern sizes in the fabric, creating a variety within seconds.

As the adventure with appliqué continues, geometric designs could again become very time consuming when the shape is stitched on the outer edge. Notice the number of corners and points in each design. Why resort to the more complicated, traditional stitching procedure when it is actually more fun and less time consuming to use another artistic approach?

Place fusing medium on the wrong side of the appliqué fabric as before. Cut the appliqué designs and fuse them in position on the garment base. Though this could be a finished project, it is advisable to stitch the edge in some manner. The choices are endless. Use rayon or metallic thread. A satin stitch with a medium to wide zigzag is appropriate. Change the width and length of the stitch to correspond to the size of the appliqué. Re-examine the shape to be stitched. Some shapes have lots of corners to miter, others are long and squiggly.

Stitch these shapes in the same manner as the leaf appliqué. Allow the outer edges to float with the stitching in the center. Consider the long squiggle and spiral shapes in the photo. Because the shapes are so narrow and long, the tendency is for the piece to shift while stitching, even though the piece is fused in place.

To prevent shifting, stitch a straight line down the center to hold it in position and return over the same line with a satin stitch.

Determine the stitch width by the proportion of the pattern width. This stitching is quick, easy, and requires half as much stitching.

New Shapes

Consider the asterisk shape. The three rows of satin stitches intersect in the center. This design is complete in seconds, whereas mitering the 18 corners would take minutes longer.

The five-point star shown is stitched using the width of the presser foot as a guide.

Double check the opening of the foot. Sometimes the needle position should be changed to the right on wider open feet to make the stitch closer to the cut edge. Other times, the foot is narrow and it's not necessary to make a change. Experiment and enjoy the freedom to change when a different design is desired for the proportion of the appliqué.

Edgestitch Appliqué

Another application for appliqué uses the edgestitching or joining foot. This foot allows the ribbon, braid, or fabric strip to align perfectly with a particular needle position. The stitching is a consistent distance from the edge of the trim as long as the trim is placed properly by the foot. Though a satin stitch may be used, the straight stitch is appropriate for finished or non-raveling edges.

Consider cutting the suede with a wavy or pinking shape. Whether scissors or a rotary cutter is used, each has its own distinctive appearance.

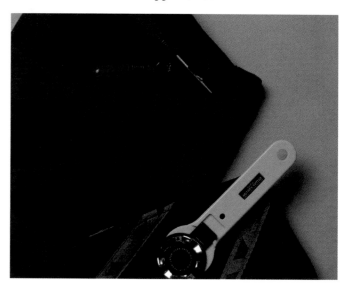

Another option is to work with woven fabrics that may take a more textured look. Cut holes in the strips using the key hole punch from the buttonhole set. Leather tools offer a large variety of hole sizes, each adding to the scheme of the pattern. Because the stitching is always visible with these versions of appliqué, utilize the variety of decorative threads available—rayon, acrylic, metallic, and lamé. Choose solid colors or variegated. Colors need not match perfectly. Occasionally a contrast adds that special touch.

When possible, use other stitches besides the satin and straight stitch. Sometimes the blanket stitch is more suitable. Play. Experiment. Sometimes it's trial and error, but it's all part of creativity and learning new techniques.

The needle is always an important factor when stitching. Choose the size needle for the weight of the fabric. Choose the eye of the needle for the type of thread you're using.

Another alternative is to change the amount of thread going through the needle. Sometimes a heavier appearing thread would make the appliqué more artistic or dimensional. Two rayon, metallic, or lamé threads will glide through the topstitching needle with ease. A slightly longer stitch length may be used, however the stitching fills in better with two threads than one. This achieves a different effect than working with a topstitching thread because two threads are softer. One of my favorite combinations is to use two variegated threads in the topstitch needle.

No matter which fabric and thread are applied, appliqué is a wondrous adventure leading to hours of enjoyment at the sewing machine. It's okay to experiment with several appliqué ideas and stitching procedures on the same project. Begin boundless exploration into the use of appliqué.

Three-Dimensional Appliqué

Spiraling makes a wonderful base for other embellishment. With the time involved to make the piecing, it's not practical to completely cover the spiraling. A portion of the garment or project could be enhanced with additional appliqué to draw attention to other areas of the garment near the face and shoulder area.

Study fabrics in your collection or at the store. So many of the fabrics available today have large designs which could be pulled from the fabric and appliquéd to a pieced or crinkled base. The tulip fabric (shown in the photos on the next page) is perfect for making three-dimensional appliqué.

Choosing the Fabric

The designs should be relatively simple, without too much detail. Remember the designs in children's coloring books? They were very plain with just a few outline markings. This is the type of fabric design that works best for three-dimensional appliqué. The designs should stand alone in the fabric without overlapping each other. Designs that overlap generally do not work well.

Depending on the position used in the project, the design should be proportionate so as not to overpower the project. The tulips are roughly 3″ wide by 4″ long. The grape section is approximately 6″ long by 5″ deep.

Different leaves were used to fill in the background. Choose designs that are in this size range. An appliqué that is too small may be difficult to stitch because of the detail.

Three to Make One

It takes three of one design to make a single dimensional appliqué. Be sure to examine the repeat in the fabric. A fabric with a large repeat may not be practical to use with this process. It's possible to substitute a fabric of comparable color for the underneath backside of the top appliqué when fabric is at a minimum or the design is not very symmetrical.

Begin with Fusing

Choose the design for the project. Place a paper-backed fusing medium on the wrong side of the fabric in the appliqué area, following the manufacturer's instruction.

Remove the paper backing from the fabric after the fabric cools. Otherwise the fabric may stick to itself from the warm fusing medium. Be aware that some fusing products must be bonded to stay on a fabric. Other products like Steam-A-Seam 2 will stick to fabric for a temporary hold. The bond becomes permanent when heat is applied.

Trim for the Base Layer

Trim on the inside line of the appliqué. Straight stitching is used in this variety of appliqué, so any excess fabric on the trim line will be visible on the finished garment.

Steam the appliqué in position on the garment. If the appliqué overlaps a shoulder seam allowance, stitch the seam allowance first.

When making flowers, apply the stems and leaves at this point. The next layer of flower appliqué will cover the ends of the stems. It's okay for the extra leaves to extend off the garment, but keep the majority of the design centered on the garment.

Straight Stitch Appliqué

For effect, straight stitch around the appliqué twice, starting and stopping in an area that will be covered by the next layer. Stitch other lines on the appliqué to add detail where desired.

Many times there are shading lines in the fabric to serve as guidelines. Choose a decorative thread like rayon or metallic. Variegated threads show wonderful shading automatically without extra effort. Use the proper needle for the type thread you've chosen. A slightly longer stitch length (2½ to 3) works best.

The Second Layer

Place fusing medium on the other two appliqué sections. Trim one to the desired size using the outside of the design as a guide. Also trim away the background

petals. This means the upper layer of appliqué is slightly larger than the one fused to the garment.

Add Batting for Dimension

To add dimension, use a layer of lightweight batting between the top layers of appliqué. The batting should be trimmed approximately 1/8″ smaller around the entire appliqué. To avoid pressing onto the iron, fuse the batting in position with the paper backing from the fusing medium or a Teflon release sheet.

Wrong Side to Wrong Side

Place the trimmed second layer, wrong side to wrong side, on the untrimmed third appliqué piece. Because the design is reversed, it may not meet exactly. In this instance, be sure the area that is open in the final position is the same coloration as the majority of the appliqué.

Fuse these layers together with the Teflon release sheet. Trim layers evenly around the appliqué. Stitch any detail lines along the open side and within the middle of the appliqué with decorative thread.

The Third Dimension

Position this upper layer of appliqué on top of the first layer fused to the garment. Because this upper layer was trimmed on the outside lines and the stitched appliqué was trimmed on the inside lines, the upper appliqué portion is slightly larger than the lower portion.

Force the outer layer to match the lower level, making the upper portion three-dimensional. Stitch around the outside edge to complete the appliqué.

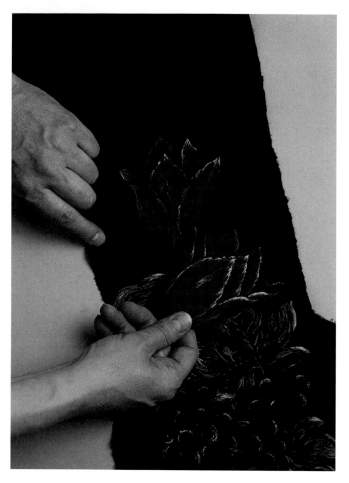

- ↝IT REQUIRES THREE OF ONE DESIGN TO MAKE A SINGLE DIMENSIONAL APPLIQUÉ.
- ↝CHOOSE A DESIGN FOR APPLIQUÉ IN PROPORTION TO THE GARMENT.
- ↝USE SHARP POINTED SCISSORS TO ACCURATELY CUT APPLIQUÉ. THE 5″ CRAFT SCISSORS WORK BEST.
- ↝REMOVE PAPER BACKING FROM FUSED FABRIC AFTER THE FABRIC COOLS.

- ↝USE AN EMBROIDERY NEEDLE WITH RAYON THREAD.
- ↝METALLICA NEEDLES WORK BEST WITH METALLIC THREAD.
- ↝A TEFLON RELEASE SHEET MAKES APPLIQUÉ EASIER AND AVOIDS PRESSING THE DESIGN ONTO THE IRON.
- ↝A SLIGHTLY LONGER STITCH LENGTH (2½ TO 3) WORKS BEST FOR DECORATIVE THREAD IN THREE-DIMENSIONAL APPLIQUÉ.

Chapter 10

Fuzzies and Tassels

*F*requently an extra touch of dimension is desired. A rhinestone, button, or sequin will not do, but something is necessary to fill a void in a space. Fuzzies and tassels qualify for this purpose. They are simple to create and the color choices are as varied as the threads available. Threads that ravel nicely, such as heavier metallic and rayon threads for the upper and lower looper in the serger, work beautifully for either technique. A combination of threads in a variety of colors produces the best design, depending on the project.

Fuzzies

To make a fuzzy, twist 10 to 20 threads together to form a cord (step 1). It is easiest to begin with several long pieces of thread, fold them in half, and then in half again.

To prevent pulling the finished fuzzy apart, use the open toe foot with a serpentine stitch, a short length and width as wide as the twisted cord, to stitch the distance eventually intended for the satin stitch (step 2). With the presser foot down, set the machine for a perfect satin stitch the width of the cord. While in reverse, stitch over the serpentine stitch to the beginning of the stitching (step 3). Set the width just a little wider and stitch forward over the previous stitches to achieve a smooth finish. Because of the bulk of threads, you may need to help the machine during the final stitching.

Step 1

Step 2   *Step 3*

Step 4

Tassels

Tassels are somewhat easier because one step is omitted. Begin with twisted threads, as with the fuzzies (step 1). Zigzag over these threads about 1/4″ (step 2). Sink the needle into the fabric, lift the presser foot, pull the upper twisted threads around to position them on top of the others, and satin stitch over the previous stitching (step 4). Widen the stitch to accommodate the double layer of threads. Trim to the desired length. Let the threads hang naturally or use your hands to mingle and separate them. Tassels have never been easier.

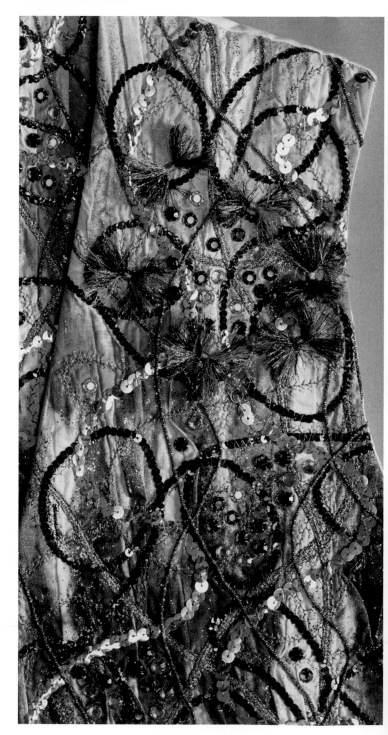

POINT OF INTEREST

⚬ ANY HEAVY SERGER TYPE THREAD OR YARN THAT RAVELS EASILY IS GREAT FOR FUZZIES AND TASSELS. TRY METALLIC, RAYON, AND RIBBON FLOSS.

⚬ TWIST THE THREADS TIGHTLY WHILE STITCHING THE SERPENTINE STITCH TO MAKE THE SMALLEST CENTER.

⚬ THE TWISTED THREAD WILL BE DOUBLED IN THE TASSEL MAKING PROCESS. PLAN ACCORDINGLY AND DO NOT MAKE THE FIRST STEP TOO LARGE.

Chapter 11

Cameo Shuffle

Sherrie Spangler

The possibilities for embellishment are endless, but occasionally you'll want a basic garment, something that can be worn as a basic yet can be transformed into a variety of looks, much like changing jewelry. An inset permits that medley of changes. A collection of buttons, a miniature quilt block, machine or hand embroidery, charted needlework, a collection of laces or embroideries, cross stitch, needlepoint, or other handwork incorporated into an inset will permit diversity in one garment.

Vests are always in fashion. They complete an ensemble and are considered an accessory. What about a vest with an interchangeable inset? A vest made from basic fabric with an inset is simple to make. Other embellishments could be incorporated into the inset.

Inset Placement

The best place to position the inset is the left shoulder in the area of a handkerchief pocket. The top of the interchangeable opening should be approximately 4½″ to 5″ from the shoulder seam on a woman's garment. The position will change on a child's garment; however, the lower edge of the opening should be higher than the lowest edge of the armscye. Take careful measurements to avoid placing the inset at the high point of the bust.

This technique can be used on the back of a jacket, the side of a handbag, as a pocket, or wherever you wish. Make sure the placement will be practical. For instance, the opening should be centered on the handbag so it is not placed towards the bottom of the bag. Sometimes this position is actually higher on the flat pattern.

Base the size and shape you use on the amount of fabric in the background area. Several oval options are shown, but perhaps a circle would show the design better. The shape may be altered and the size enlarged or reduced. Determine how much working area there is, taking seam allowances into consideration. There must be at least 1½″ on all sides of the opening for the interchangeable idea to work properly.

Mock Corded Piping Fabric

Select a fabric to use as a mock corded piping. Contrasting fabric will show definition, while matching fabric makes a more subtle difference. The wrong side of the fabric may be used when a slight change is desired. This idea works beautifully with denim, which is great on both sides. When a contrasting fabric is difficult to find, perhaps the wrong side of the fabric would be more suitable for the mock corded piping.

The finished opening looks as though much time was spent constructing corded piping, but the basic concept is simply a facing. To make the mock cording, cut an 8″ square of the facing fabric. Position the right side of the cording fabric on the right side of the fashion fabric. These stages are shown on the handbag.

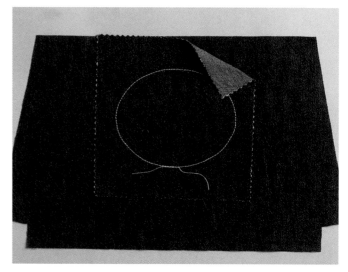

Marking the Hole

Use a washable marker or pencil to mark the exact size of the opening on the wrong side of the facing fabric. Mark the exact size of the opening on the mock cording piece. This technique does not add to or take away from the size of the opening.

Stitch, Trim, and Press

Use a short stitch length (1½ to 2) to stitch around the oval. Overlap the ending with beginning stitches to secure and avoid bulk.

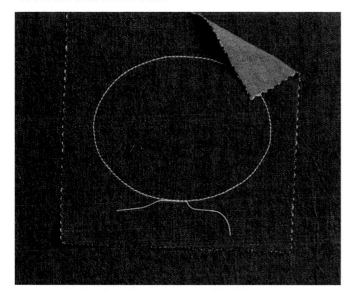

Trim to 1/16″ but no wider than 1/8″.

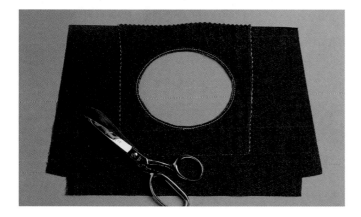

Turn the cording fabric through the hole to allow just an edge (no more the 1/8″) of the cording fabric to show.

Stitch in the ditch with the edgestitching foot to hold the cording in place.

The edgestitching foot works better than the open toe foot because the tiny edging on the foot aligns perfectly with the corded area. The narrow trimmed seam allowance fills the cording area, making the ridge look as though there is corded piping in the area.

Steam press the opening to maintain the shape. Trim the mock piping facing to 6½″ square. This is the size all future insets should be.

Center the Inset Over the Opening

On the wrong side of the hole, center an embellished square over the opening.

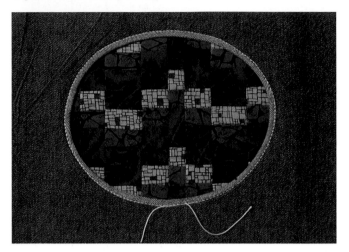

The square should be 1/4″ smaller all the way around (6″ square), forming a graded area. Trim as necessary.

Place fusible web between the wrong side of the inset and the fleece. Fuse them together using a wet press cloth and the wool setting on a steam iron. This step will form a permanent pocket for other embellishments. The mock cording has the illusion of corded piping though there is none.

Stages on a Garment Shoulder

The instructions change slightly when the inset is positioned on a garment.

Melanie Gardiner

Choose a fusible interfacing that is light and soft, not stiff or bulky. French Fuse™ is a recommended weight. Cut fusible interfacing at least 1″ larger than the facing section. Place fusible interfacing over the complete mock cording section to hold the interchangeable pocket in place. Fusible interfacing replaces the fusible web and fleece used in the handbag. Use the wool setting with heavy steam to hold the interfacing in place. Trim the excess mock cording fabric, inset fabric, and interfacing along the vest cutting lines of the neck, armscye, and shoulder. The lower edge of the interfacing is fused to the body of the garment. This interfacing prevents other insets from falling between the fashion fabric and lining and forms the pocket.

Determine the pocket size formed by these steps. This is the size for the base fabric to be used for future insets. To have pretty finished edges on the insets, it is wise to mark the opening size on the base fabric, allowing more than ample around the edges. Once the embellishment is complete, trim to the size of the pocket.

- MARK THE OPENING SIZE ON THE BASE FABRIC AND EMBELLISH GALORE.
- BUTTONS AND SILK RIBBON EMBROIDERY MAKE AN ELEGANT EVENING BAG.
- BEADS, SEQUINS, RHINE-STONES, TRADITIONAL OR CONTEMPORARY PIECING, APPLIQUÉ, HEIRLOOM SEWING, PINTUCKING, COUCHING, CRINKLING, CHARTED NEEDLEWORK, MACHINE EMBROIDERY, CROSS STITCH, NEEDLEPOINT—AND MORE—MAY BE USED IN SMALL PORTIONS.
- WHEN CHOOSING FABRIC FOR MOCK CORDED PIPING, AVOID FIBERS THAT RAVEL.
- USE A SHORT STITCH LENGTH TO STITCH THE OPENING.
- THE CUT OPENING IS THE SAME SIZE AS THE FINISHED OPENING. NOTHING IS ADDED AND NOTHING TAKEN AWAY WITH SEAM ALLOWANCES.

Evelyn Dix

Chapter 12

Pintucking

PINTUCKING: A SMALL, FLAT FOLD
STITCHED INTO A GARMENT. A STITCH
THAT PRODUCES TUCK EFFECTS AS A
SPECIAL NEEDLE SEWS FOLDS IN THE
FABRIC.

Classic pintucks are formed by folding a specific amount of fabric and hand or machine stitching a slight distance from the fold. Double needles and pintucking feet make it fast and easy to produce rows of pintucks with uniformity and minimal effort.

Pintuck Feet

Most machines have a variety of pintucking feet available. They have grooves on the bottom varying in width and number. The wider the groove, the larger the tuck. The narrower the groove, the smaller the tuck. Larger grooved feet make fewer tucks, whereas smaller, closer grooves have more tucks.

Determine what size pintucks are desired before choosing the foot. My favorite is the seven-groove pintucking foot for most work, however I do use the three-groove foot for larger tucks or small corded piping. Any of the pintucking feet will accomplish the texture techniques shown here.

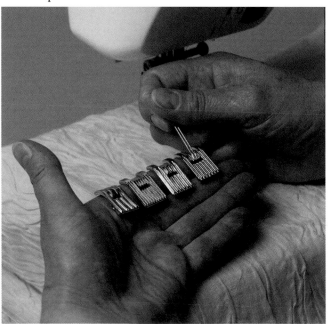

The Double Needle

After selecting the pintucking foot, determine the corresponding double needle. A double needle consists of two needles attached to a single shank. These needles will fit in any zigzag machine that threads from the front and has a wide hole in the throat plate.

The numbers on the needle package relate to the millimeter distance between the two needles and the size of the needle. There are a variety of double needle sizes available for an assortment of fabrics or threads. Be sure to choose the one appropriate for your needs.

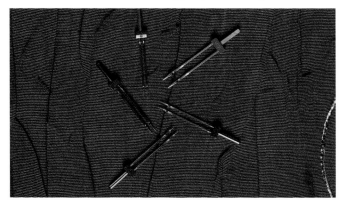

Somewhere in your sewing manuals there is a chart showing what size needle goes with which foot. The easiest tip to remember is that the correct needle should match the grooves on the foot.

The ridge in the foot should not cause the needles to spread, nor should it push them closer together. On a larger grooved foot, the needle should center in the middle of the groove.

Before you begin stitching, decide what kind of thread will help you achieve the desired result. Rayon or cotton embroidery thread, metallic, lamé, silk, and acrylic thread work beautifully in double needles for pintucks.

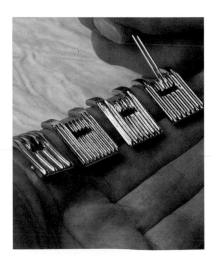

The Bobbin

Fill the bobbin with all-purpose thread and have several filled bobbins available to reload the machine when one runs out. Pintucking is another instance when much thread is used in the bobbin. The bobbin has to connect with both top threads, making the wrong side a zigzag stitching. Always be prepared to reload the machine to avoid a break in the stitching. Whenever possible, try to reload the bobbin at the beginning of a seam. This area will eventually be trimmed away.

Threading the Machine

Generally the thread on the left spool holder feeds the left needle and the thread on the right spool holder feeds the right needle. This threading procedure works on machines with vertical spool holders. Many machines today have horizontal spool holders. The best advice is to refer to your machine manual for the proper way to thread your machine.

Troubleshooting

Always allow the threads to pass freely from the spool to the first thread guide. Don't let the thread on one spool holder rub against the other spool, or a twist will form and the threads will break. If there isn't a guide on the machine to prevent this problem, position the spools on the holder so that one thread feeds from the front of the machine and the other spool feeds from the back.

When only one spool of thread is available, wind a bobbin of that thread for the additional needle. If both the bobbin and spool are placed on the same spool holder, place one on the holder feeding from the front and the other feeding from the back. There will be slight tension from the spools to the first thread guide. This will not change the stitch quality, but will prevent the spool from spinning on the spool holder.

Stitch Length

Experiment with stitch length. There is no special rule to follow for combining fabric, thread, needle, and foot in creating different effects. A longer stitch makes a softer tuck, a shorter stitch produces a more ridged tuck. A medium stitch length is a good place to start testing.

Sometimes it is appropriate to tighten the tension to form the tucks desired. On machines with an extra fin-ger on the bobbin case, thread the hole in the finger to tighten the tension.

Pintucking in the Round

It is relatively simple to make pintucks on long strips of fabric. Often, when sewing rows of pintucking, the restarting process can cause a problem with needles unthreading and threads jamming. To avoid these problems I like to pintuck in the round, a technique I learned in an heirloom sewing class taught by Mildred Turner.

To begin, cut the fabric several inches longer than the desired length or at least the distance around the free arm of the sewing machine (usually 15″). Cut the fabric twice as wide as the desired amount to allow for shrinkage in the pintucking process. Be sure all the edges are straight and on grain. Plan for the pintucks to stitch on the lengthwise grain for the best tucks. Tucks stitched on the crossgrain usually stretch, making them ripple.

If the selvage is trimmed from the fabric, test for the grain line by pulling the fabric along grain. The side with the most stretch is the crossgrain. The side that will not stretch is the length.

Forming the Tube of Fabric

Form a tube of fabric by overlapping the crossgrain edges about 1″ with the cut edge facing you.

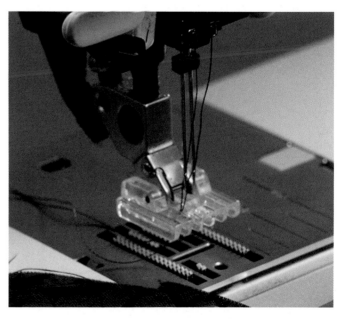

The under edge at the grain line should extend 1/8″ to compensate for the stitching process. Stitch the center of the overlap, forming a tube.

Begin the stitching process on the overlapped seam.

Make all changes on this seam allowance. Stitch completely around the tube, using the cut edge as a guide to stitch straight. This first stitching should be at least 1/2″ from the cut edge to avoid stretching. It is important that this seam be very straight and accurate, as it determines how perfect all future rows will be.

As the foot approaches the beginning stitches, the first pintuck will align with the selected groove under the foot. All future rows will be stitched with one of these grooves as a guide. This is how to produce rows and rows of parallel pintucks. The outside edge of the foot can also serve as an additional guide when more distance between the tucks is desired.

Continue stitching around the fabric tube, using the grooves as a guide.

One groove can be used throughout the project or many different patterns could evolve, depending on the result you want. I used to establish patterns of three rows close together with a single row a little further apart.

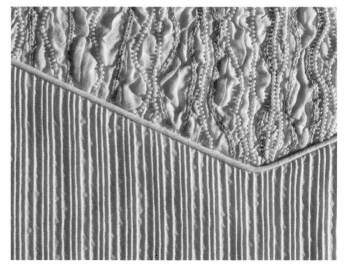

This was fun but too rigid. Try a symmetrical system or an irregular design, as shown in the photos.

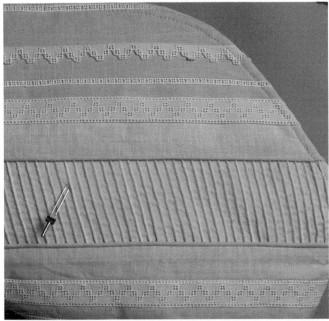

Decorative Stitches

Experiment with a few decorative stitches and the double needle pintucks.

Be careful to test the stitch width to avoid breaking needles. There are buttons on most machines for this purpose. I usually double check my stitch width by hand, walking the machine through the stitch. No matter what, it doesn't take long to realize if the stitch width is too wide—there will be two broken needles flying from the machine.

The feather stitch is excellent in the double needle.

Continue the pintucking procedure throughout the fabric tube. You may find it unnecessary to use the grooves close to the needle as guides. The overlapping decorative stitch fills in with decoration. Be aware that decorative stitches in pintucking cause the fabric to draw up almost double in width and slightly in length. Plan to begin with ample fabric.

Use your imagination to create. Try figured fabrics as well as solids. The design in the fabric will become more elongated. Change colors and types of thread to form artistic strips. Use variegated thread for subtle color changes. Experiment—things will start to happen and new ideas will arise.

Open the Tube

When the pintucking is complete, cut along the original straight stitched overlapped line. There will be some waste along the overlap area. Since this method is the quickest way to produce many rows of perfect pintucks, the waste is small.

Corded Pintucks

Corded pintucks have a lightweight cording or heavy thread enclosed in each fold. Pearl cotton, gimpe, or other heavier thread may be used for this purpose. For extra color, choose colored thread that shadows through a sheer fabric.

The thread may just fill the fold without any visible color change. The purpose of the additional thread is to stiffen the tuck, giving it a more ridged, defined appearance.

Most machines have an extra hole in the throat plate or an additional foot to produce corded pintucks.

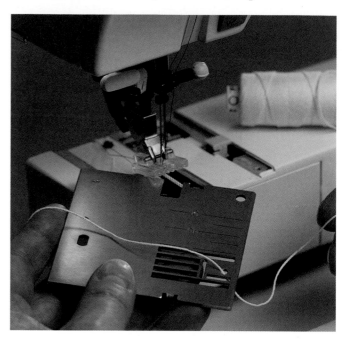

Refer to your machine manual for tips on your machine. Slide the gimpe through the hole and replace the throat plate, being sure the gimpe flows freely through the machine.

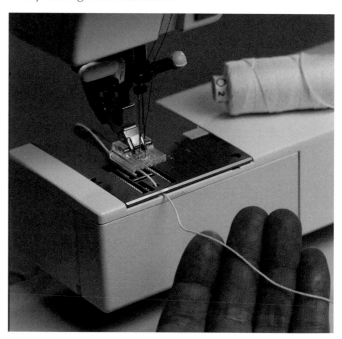

Stitch with the double needle as before. The difference here is that the cording will be sandwiched between the bobbin thread and the wrong side of the fabric, producing a much heavier and rigid pintuck than before.

Sometimes this is the shadowing and texture desired rather than the softer pintucks. The fabric and threads you choose determine the new design.

Variety

Pintucking in the round makes pintucking much simpler with uncomplicated rows of perfectly parallel pintucks. But many times that method makes too many or takes too long to cover a certain portion of a project. So why not meander all over the fabric using the same feet and needles? It covers more territory, makes wonderful intersections, forms little framed areas for other embellishments, and takes less time.

Esther Morford

Just as updating other types of needlework requires a few extra tips and tricks, so does pintucking. Because there is no way to know how much fabric the tucking will use, begin with a piece at least one third larger than the expected finished size. The fabric should be relatively soft to form the tucks. If the fabric is very sheer or soft, spray starch and press it first to add body. The starch prevents lightweight fabric from gathering in the grooves of the foot and forming large or uneven tucks.

Pintucks can be corded or not. They can be sewn with any type of thread mentioned before. The needle size and width distance can vary according to the type of fabric and thread for the desired finished appearance. A good starting point is a 2.0 size 80 needle with the seven-groove pintuck foot.

It is always easier to begin and end on the edge of the fabric. There are no untidy ends to contend with. Be certain the presser foot is completely on the fabric before beginning. The larger hole in the throat plate sometimes tends to pull the fabric into the machine.

Keeping just enough fabric under the foot to cover the hole prevents a problem from occurring. Though it is fine to mark the fabric with wavy lines, experiment with stitching without the lines. These stitching lines should be slightly wavy, not very deep curves. More rounded curves cover a good portion of bias on the fabric. Prevent stretching the fabric by allowing the machine to feed the fabric as it sews. Avoid pushing, pulling, or tugging at the fabric in any way.

Meander over the fabric to an edge. Stop with the needle in the up position. Lift the presser foot and pull the fabric about 1˝ to prevent the next row from gathering at the beginning. Lower the presser foot, aligning the previous row of stitching in one of the grooves. Continue stitching perfectly parallel rows of wavy pintucks. Sew several rows that are parallel but not necessarily evenly spaced, then form another wavy line to intersect the previous one. The overlapping areas are always different shapes and sizes, depending on the angles they intersect. These unexpected designer touches can add to the artistic arrangement of the composition.

The spaces formed where there is no stitching are perfect little framed areas for monograms, decorative stitch combinations, embroidery, or enlarged programmed stitch designs. Not every area needs to be filled with a design, but a few of the larger areas warrant a cluster of added stitches. It is the perfect place to show off the features of your machine. Experiment. Think of the fun you are going to have!

• USE THE DOUBLE NEEDLE THAT CORRESPONDS TO THE FABRIC AND THREAD TYPE.

• SHORTEN THE STITCH LENGTH FOR MORE RIDGED TUCKS. LENGTHEN THE STITCH LENGTH FOR A FLATTER APPEARANCE.

• TO RIP DOUBLE NEEDLE STITCHING, REMOVE THE BOBBIN THREAD AND THE NEEDLE THREADS WILL FALL AWAY FROM THE FABRIC.

• A TRIPLE NEEDLE IS STITCHED IN THE SAME MANNER AS A DOUBLE NEEDLE. THE DIFFERENCE IS THAT THERE ARE THREE VISIBLE DECORATIVE THREADS RATHER THAN TWO.

• ALWAYS USE THE SAME TYPE THREAD IN EACH NEEDLE. NEVER MIX THREADS IN THE SAME NEEDLE, BUT IT IS OKAY TO MIX THREADS IN THE SAME PROJECT.

Triple needle with metallic threads. Use the width of the presser foot to sew perfectly parallel lines.

Chapter 13

Heirloom Sewing

Heirloom sewing converts French hand sewing to machine methods using fine laces, trims, and fabrics, creating a treasured possession to be handed down in a family for generations.

Heirloom sewing is often considered too fussy, with frilly laces, trims, tucks, and ribbons. When used conservatively, a small amount of lace can make a very tailored suit more stylish. Add a row of embroidery trims to a basic blouse for a more feminine touch. It is not necessary to have rows and rows of lace. It's nice, but not necessary to create an heirloom ensemble.

With the colors and fabrics available today, it's easy to combine the old art with modern techniques to create many different types of texture. Consider the possibilities of dyeing, piecing, and combining heirloom with crinkling. The end product could be contemporary or something from the past.

Lace to Lace

Before beginning to sew lace to lace, spray starch and iron the lace to shrink and stabilize it. The extra body will simplify the process. For best results, use a smaller machine needle such as 60/8 or 65/9. Change the needle frequently to maintain a sharp point. When sewing with fine laces and trims, use 100% cotton 60 or 70 weight thread to eliminate bulk. There is generally no right or wrong side to laces.

To attach flat straight edges together—insertion, beading, or edging—butt the straight edges and use the edgestitching foot to align the laces perfectly. This foot makes it easy to stitch equally the entire length of the laces.

Do not overlap. Zigzag over the lace headings using a medium to narrow zigzag stitch. Start testing with a medium stitch width and length. The stitch width should be wide enough to cover the heading yet not so wide it closes the lace. The stitch length should be short enough to hold the laces together without making a satin stitch. Machines and laces vary, so always test stitch first.

Where necessary, match lace patterns. For a different look, combine a variety of patterns rather than using a single pattern. Create a design that pleases you without matching each piece of lace and the design.

Once the stitch is set, it's easy to combine rows of laces together with little effort. The foot aligns the proper distance and you guide the lace. Remember to adjust the machine each time a different lace is used. Sew with a smooth even speed rather than top speed.

Entredeux and Beading

Entredeux and beading are placed between rows of lace and other trims to add strength. They are embroideries with a definite right and wrong side. The rounded smooth side is the right side, while the rough side is the wrong side. If you have to look more than three seconds to determine which is the right side, don't worry about it. Sometimes it's very difficult to see the difference.

Trim batiste from only one side at a time to avoid twisting and turning the entredeux.

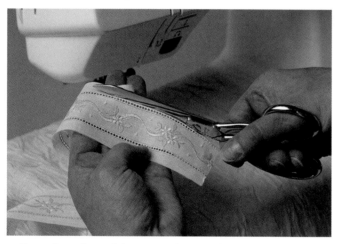

Butt the edge of the entredeux or beading to the lace with the edgestitching foot and zigzag these edges together.

Setting the Machine

The machine should be set so that the zig goes over the heading and the zag goes in a hole of the entredeux or beading. Use the shape or size of the holes as a guide to set the machine width and length. Machines and laces will always vary, so test before starting the project. Avoid having the needle touch the trim rather than go in the hole. You paid for these holes so they should be visible in the finished garment.

Trim the extra batiste from the remaining edge and continue to add more lace or decorative trim. Build the laces and embroideries until the piece is large enough to cut the garment section.

Decorative Embroidery Trims

Trims consist of embroidery designs stitched on batiste. They are used with insertions with raw edges on both sides and edgings with a finished decorative edge and a raw edge. The raw edges will ravel and they have a definite right and wrong side. The right side is raised and shiny, while the wrong side is flat and dull.

There are several ways to attach these components together. My favorite is to place right sides together and stitch with the beading on top and the insertion underneath. Use the edgestitch foot to stitch the most accurate seam next to the beading. Press towards the beading to keep it rounded.

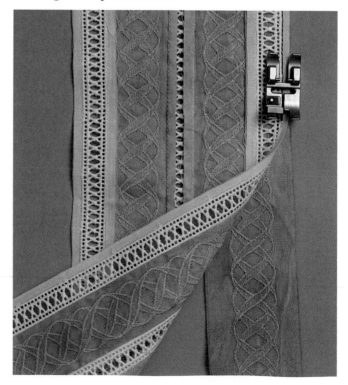

Rolling the Edge

Another way to connect fabric to embroidery begins by rolling the edge. Before attaching these pieces, zigzag over the cut edge with a narrow stitch to roll the cut edge. The process begins by aligning the cut edge with the edgestitching foot on the left side of the bar. Zig in the fabric, zag over the edge. The stitch is set to accommodate the zig. Zagging over the edge causes the raw edge of the fabric or trim to roll, which prevents raveling and gives a strong edge for adding an attachment.

To attach a trim with the rolled edge to entredeux or beading, butt the two edges against either side of the edgestitching foot. Zig over the rolled edge and zag into the holes of the trimmed beading or entredeux. This finish gives a very flat look from the front with no seam allowances on the back.

Raveling Fabrics for a Flat Finish

Using fabrics that ravel, such as handkerchief linen, can cause another problem. The seams could pull apart with stress. To avoid this, make a corded pintuck 1/2″ from the cut edge then trim to the tuck. Roll the edge as before except the zig goes in the fabric and the zag goes over the pintuck. The lightweight embroidery thread will not make this finish bulky, rather flat and finished. With matching thread, the stitching is almost invisible.

The basics of heirloom sewing are very easy. Add a little lace to your sewing for a different look.

POINT OF INTEREST

- USE A SMALL NEEDLE SIZE 60/8 OR 65/5 FOR HEIRLOOM SEWING.
- THE EDGESTITCHING FOOT IS INVALUABLE WITH HEIRLOOM SEWING.

- 60 OR 70 WEIGHT 100% COTTON THREAD IS THE FINEST THREAD TO USE. THE STITCHING BLENDS WITH THE THREADS OF THE LACE AND EMBROIDERIES.

Chapter 14
Choosing the Fabric

Various fabrics may be used for piecework. The cotton weights for quilt making are easy to find and the color selection is enormous. Shop at quilt stores where the choices range from calico to very modern prints, plaids, and stripes. Many fabrics have a lamé print for extra focus.

The concept to remember when selecting fabric is that the fabric does not need to match perfectly. Contrast in color—as well as sizes of print—makes a very effective design. Even a color you wouldn't use in a large piece can be used successfully in very narrow strips. The contrast will cause the colors to bounce and complement each other.

True, but very difficult to believe sometimes, is the fact that the fabric is going to be cut up rather than used in a large full piece. If you come from a garment sewing background where the suit or skirt fabric was to match the blouse fabric perfectly, it will require deliberation for perfect coordination. Piecing requires the fabrics to be slightly off in various combinations for the design to work.

Purchase one yard pieces of fabrics when selecting colors to add to your stash. When a fabric is most desirable for the stockpile, buy more than one yard. Remember, this piece of fabric may enter into several projects during its lifetime. If the colors are among your favorites, that combination will appear again. Purchase the fabric when you find it because it may not be there on a future trip to the store.

On a recent teaching trip, I discovered a wonderful piece of fabric in the shop. Rather than put the piece aside to purchase immediately, I waited until packing my suitcases to begin making my purchases. Discovering that my bolt was missing, I asked the salesperson about it. She had sold "my fabric" to one of the students in class. Of course, the salesperson was unaware that I wanted the fabric. But she did quote me from class, "Remember, you said to get it while you can, even if you don't know what you want to do with it because it may not be there the next time you go to the store!" Sometimes we have to eat our words.

Because the full width of fabric is cut for this strip piecing technique, my preference is to use fabric the width of the bolt rather than fat quarters or smaller amounts of fabric. Many times those small portions of fabric are just enough to frustrate me when I go to the cutting mat. So consider this when choosing fabric. It's always nicer to have a little extra than to force creations from a limited supply of fabric.

Besides cottons, many other fabrics work nicely in piecing. Lamé, whether knit or woven (interface first for added strength and stability), lightweight silks like douppioni or raw silk, wool or rayon challis, sueded rayon or silk, moiré taffeta, polyester or silk jacquards, velvet or velveteen are excellent choices. The combinations are endless.

The variety of fabrics available today makes it fun to create a masterpiece of mixed texture with textiles. The interpretation of combinations becomes a creation of the creator. They are design choices.

Stabilize Lightweight Fabrics

Always interface any soft fabrics like lamé, sueded rayon, or sheers before including them in a piecing project. The interfacing will stabilize and give support to the fragile fabric, causing less wear and tear.

Always interface lamé from the wrong side or interfacing side to avoid a catastrophe. The heat of the iron will cause the nylon threads of a woven lamé to melt, leaving the metallic threads behind. A hot iron will shift the metallic color layer on a knitted lamé.

Chapter 15

Lattice Piecing

I may never make a quilt, but I adore the combinations of fabrics, colors, and designs used in quilts today. Many of the techniques used in quilting also translate well to sewing garments and accessories. I want to try as many of the piecing patterns as I possibly can, using them on a smaller scale than in quilt making for a bed or the wall.

Many designers make templates or puzzle pieces for their quilt and build them into a wonderful larger piece. Others have quicker ideas. They take fine fabric, cut it up, and sew it together in strips. Then they may cut it and sew it back together again. By shuffling the pieces as they are restitched, these designers form unique patterns. This type of sewing can be used to create either traditional piecing or contemporary designs. The modern term for this process of cutting, sewing, cutting, sewing is known as quick piecing.

Sewing has monopolized much of my time. Whenever possible, I take classes from other teachers as inspiration and to enhance my skills. I always add my taste to their concept. One inspiring teacher is Jude Larzelere. Her techniques are used in my garment for *Statements 1992*. I changed the technique so drastically that Jude didn't recognize her own technique when she saw my garment.

The First Cut

Because this piecing shrinks tremendously, you should begin with a base fabric at least 1½ times the finished size. The base fabric shown here is crinkled, but it could be flat too.

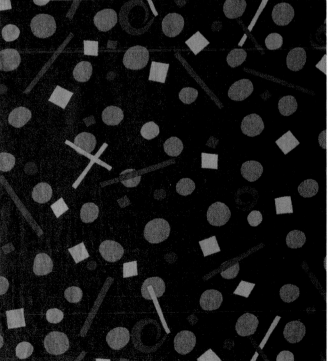

Cut the base fabric lengthwise every 2″ to 4″. Insert cut strips approximately 1″ to 2″ wide, using 1/4″ seam allowances. Press the seams towards the darker fabric. When the base fabric is crinkled, press towards the inserted piece.

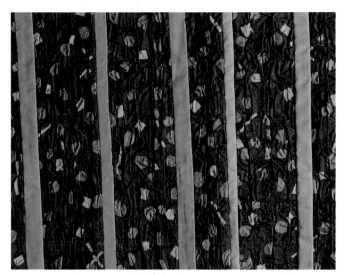

The Second Cut

The next cutting is diagonal lines from one direction. This is not a true bias, but somewhere in the general area. The cutting lines are spaced approximately 3″ to 4″ apart.

The insert strips should be slightly narrower than the first insert strips. As the strips are inserted, shift the base piece up or down so the previous seams don't match. The first narrow strips will be chopped into different shapes and sizes to form new dimensions. Press towards the inserted strip.

The Third Cut

Continuing to the third insert strip, cut the base fabric in the opposite diagonal direction. This is not a true bias. The cutting lines are spaced about 2½″ to 5″ apart. The inserted strips are narrower than the previous strips. This section could be entredeux beading. Notice the difference the color makes with and without ribbon. Again, as the strips are stitched back together, avoid matching the cross sections. The base fabric and added strips will continue to be cut into bits.

The Fourth Cut

The final insert is the smallest. The base fabric is cut at several angles, but none of the cuts intersect each other. The narrower the strip, the more difficult it is to keep them even.

ric. The base could be crinkled figured fabric with additional solid and/or figured fabrics.

Let your imagination run free. Add a strip of lamé. Use an embroidery insertion. There are no set rules.

The narrow beading sews in perfectly because the edge-stitching foot guides the needle position. Again, notice the difference with and without ribbon. Just as before, the sections are not aligned as stitched.

This piecing technique is beautiful with solid color fabric as well as a combination solid and figured fab-

Extra Tips for Lattice Piecing

Always begin with more fabric than you think you will need. It's possible for lattice piecing to shrink in one direction and grow in another, depending on the width of the strips inserted.

Black is an excellent base to use with a variety of high contrast strips. A tone-on-tone design does not show the technique as well as accent colors for the different inserts. Pastels are as pretty as jewel tones. Vary the colors in the design.

A 1/2″ or wider ribbon with ruffled edges could be used instead of an inserted strip for the first cut. To maintain a straight line, machine baste the ribbon with a clear thread on base fabric. Couch in position using a decorative stitch or combination of stitches on the machine.

When a solid color is used for the base, couch heavier metallic threads or narrow ribbons as opposed to the first cutting. Label the strips when cutting to maintain the proper sequence.

Place strips at varying distances. They may be parallel or slightly off. Change the angle of cuts for different looks. A combination of couching and embroidery can be very elegant or sporty.

Try to accentuate breaks in color. Don't match strips at seams. To prevent stretching the fabric on the bias, always place the accent color on top. Press the seams toward the darker strip unless the bulk of crinkling or beading prevents pressing flat. I have very successfully used three cuts for lattice piecing instead of four.

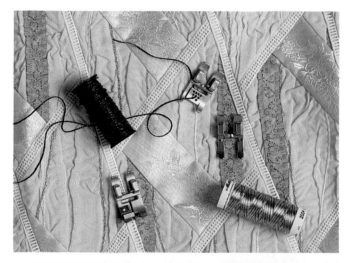

Charleen Pollman

Chapter 16
Cutting the Strips

With modern conveniences like the rotary cutter, it's easy to cut many strips in a short time. Rather than cutting one layer of fabric at a time, fold the fabric selvage to selvage crossgrain. This means all strips will be 45˝ long (the width of the fabric). Be certain the fabric is not twisted in any way, but flat from the fold to the two selvages. The selvages should be perfectly even.

Fold the folded edge to the two selvages, being careful to avoid any twists or wrinkles in the fabric.

Regardless of how the fabric was cut at the store, be certain the fabric is flat from folded edge to selvage. Sometimes fabric may be off grain. It may be impossible to straighten the fabric. Consequently, straight strips are more important than straight grain.

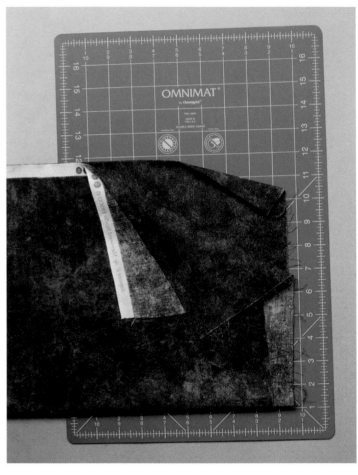

Cutting Tools

Use a rotary cutter, cutting mat, and see-through ruler at least 3˝ wide and 14˝ long to straighten the fabric and cut the strips. Accuracy is important in the cutting. Use the ruler as a guide rather than guessing.

Align a right angle marking on the ruler with the folded edge of the fabric. With one hand on the rotary cutter, the blade next to the ruler, and the other hand on the ruler to hold it in position, straighten the uneven edges of the fabric.

Turn the fabric around and position the ruler on the fabric so that an increment of the ruler is even with the previously cut edge. Using a sharp blade, cut the strip with one stroke. Using a sawing motion or a nicked or dull blade will cause jagged edges. A clean finish and straight edge is most desirable.

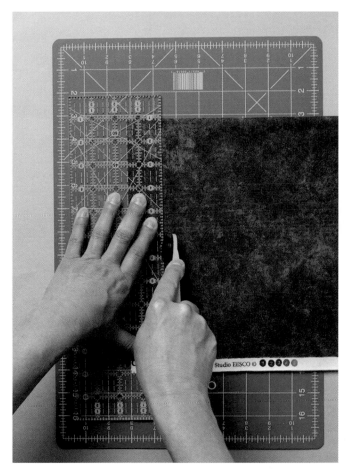

When the strip is opened it should be perfectly straight when cut with these instructions. Folding the fabric improperly or allowing the ruler to slip while cutting will cause the cut strip to look like the photo below.

Width of Strips

Mixed widths from 3/4″ to 4″ make an effective design. Most quilting rulers have 1/4″ marking. Use them as a guide for varying widths of strips. It is not necessary to make all strips identical in width. Allow 1/4″ on each side of the strip for seam allowances. Therefore, the width of the finished sewn strip is 1/2″ narrower than the cut strip. A 3/4″ cut strip will leave 1/4″ visible. This is a very narrow strip. It will take some time to build a project from 3/4″ strips and requires more fabric.

Cut some strips 3/4″ when a minimal amount of a color is desired. Use these narrow strips for accent colors. Cut other strips 1″, 1¼″, 1½″, 1¾″, 2″, 2¼″, 2½″ and so on, depending on the design in the fabric or the amount of color desired. The narrower the strips are cut, the more strips are necessary to complete the project.

POINT OF INTEREST

➤ FOLDING THE FABRIC IMPROPERLY WILL CAUSE THE CUT STRIP TO LOOK CROOKED.
➤ FASTEN LITTLE PIECES OF FINE SANDPAPER TO THE RULER WITH DOUBLE STICK TAPE TO PREVENT SLIDING WHILE CUTTING.
➤ ALLOW 1/4″ ON EACH SIDE OF THE CUT STRIP FOR SEAM ALLOWANCES.
➤ USE NARROW STRIPS FOR ACCENT COLORS.
➤ ALLOW EXTRA FABRIC FOR SEAM ALLOWANCES ON NARROW STRIPS.

Chapter 17

Sewing the Strips for Spiral Piecing

*L*ay the strips on a surface in a sequence pleasing to the eye.

There are no set rules to follow. Use this book as a guide to begin. Make some strips close to the same width and others wide combined with narrow. Use a very wide piece as a filler so the design is not so busy. Occasionally use a very bright or contrast fabric in a narrow strip. Consider light, medium, and dark fabric combinations. Prints as opposed to solid color combinations add variation. The most effective designs in piecing use many combinations of sets which *do not match*. Be certain the strips on the outside edges look good next to each other. They will be stitched together in the spiraling process.

Measuring the Sets

After you decide which strip goes where in the group or set, it is nice to know how wide the set will become once it is sewn together. One option is to use a calculator to determine the width, subtracting the 1/4″ seam allowances. This could be very confusing.

The simplest way to measure is to use my two finger addition method.

Position the strips on a ruler, beginning at one end and butting each strip in the set together. The strips should not overlap nor should there be space between them. Using two fingers to measure (each finger is considered 1/2″, two fingers 1″), measure the amount of seam allowance in the set. Subtract this number from the width of the butted strips. The result may not be exact, but it will be close. It is that simple. It does not take a mathematician to do the figuring.

Which Presser Foot to Use

Though every machine on the market has a 1/4″ foot for piecing, it is not necessary to use that foot in strip piecing.

The most desirable width for the seam allowance is 1/4″, however I sometimes change my mind and wish I had cut a strip narrower or slightly wider. Sewing with the basic foot allows the freedom to move the needle position to the left or right to accommodate slight changes in the width of the fabric.

Using the 1/4″ foot does not allow needle movement from the center position. Any change will cause needle breakage. Experiment and use the foot that is most convenient.

Easy Trick for Narrow Strips

When narrow strips (3/4″ and 1″) are stitched, it is very easy for the stitched strips to become uneven. Sometimes the ruler slips while cutting so the strip is not perfectly even or the cut edge moves from the side of the presser foot while stitching. To avoid the problem of irregular finished strips, use the left side of the presser foot as a guide and move the needle position to the desired width from the left. Position the presser foot next to the previously stitched row.

Leaning the presser foot against the ridge from the former row, stitch the new seam. It does not matter if the seam allowance is perfectly even. The important thing is that the visible strip of fabric is straight and uniform.

POINT OF INTEREST

⤳ USE AN 80 NEEDLE ON COTTON WEIGHT FABRIC.

⤳ THE LIFE OF A NEEDLE IS ABOUT EIGHT SEWING HOURS. CHANGE NEEDLES AS NECESSARY.

⤳ CHOOSE A BASIC COLOR THREAD (BEIGE, GRAY, BLACK, OR NAVY) THAT WILL WORK WITH ALL COLORS IN THE PROJECT. ALWAYS USE THE COLOR CLOSE TO THE LIGHTEST STRIP IN THE PROJECT.

⤳ THE THREAD SHOULD CORRESPOND TO THE WEIGHT OF THE FABRIC USED. GENERALLY, MY FAVORITE THREAD IS METROSENE PLUS POLYESTER THREAD. THERE MAY BE INSTANCES WHERE 100% COTTON SEWING THREAD OR 100% FINE COTTON EMBROIDERY (60 WEIGHT) THREAD WORKS BETTER.

⤳ FILL SEVERAL BOBBINS BEFORE STARTING A PROJECT. AS ONE RUNS OUT, RELOAD THE CASE AND CONTINUE SEWING. THERE IS NO NEED TO PULL THE PROJECT AWAY FROM THE MACHINE.

⤳ USE A SMALLER STITCH LENGTH SUCH AS 2.0.

⤳ BE CERTAIN THE STRIPS ON THE OUTSIDE EDGES LOOK GOOD NEXT TO EACH OTHER.

⤳ TRY TO HAVE WIDER STRIPS ON THE OUTSIDE EDGE.

Sewing the Sets

Position the strips of one set to the left of the machine. Sew strips together in pairs using a 2.0 stitch length with the narrow strip on top or up. Continue from one pair to another without trimming the threads.

This will also keep the pairs in sequence. There is no need to backstitch. The smaller stitch length, combined with overlapping seams, prevents the stitching from pulling out.

Pressing the Seams

Press the seams together first to bury the stitches in the fabric. Then press both seam allowances toward the darker fabric.

Continue the pairs process until the set is complete. Though it may seem practical to sew all strips together before pressing, the finished appearance is far more precise by sewing in pairs. Fewer extra tucks form in the pressing process. Avoid making an arched shape strip rather than a straight strip.

Width of Strips

The long strips stitched together or set should be at least 7″ to 16″ wide for the spiraling to work easily. Each set need not be exactly the same width. The wider the set, the easier it is to continue with the spiraling procedure on the sewing machine. There is no need to have a set wider than 16″.

Square the Strip

Using a see-through ruler and a rotary cutter, square both ends of the strip.

Accuracy is important. Beginning with a right angle makes future steps more precise. A crooked edge and seam cause future seams to be off slightly.

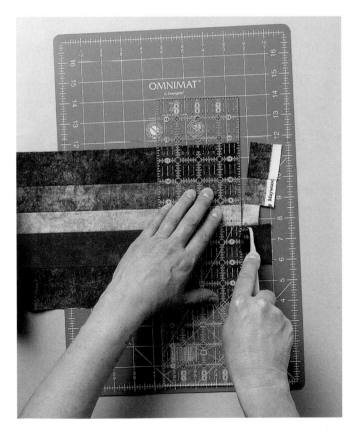

Begin to Spiral

With the sewn strips lying flat on a surface, fold one corner over to the side to form a bias angle. Folding some strips to the right and others to the left adds variety to the finished project.

When all the strips are folded in the same direction, the diagonal is the same direction. By placing some folds to the right and others to the left, mirror images form.

- SEW WITH THE NARROW STRIP UP OR NEXT TO THE PRESSER FOOT.
- ALWAYS PRESS A SEAM BEFORE ADDING ANOTHER STRIP TO PREVENT LITTLE TUCKS FROM FORMING.

Make the Pivot

Place a pin in the 1/4″ seam at the corner.

Pivot the corner to align the longer straight edges. This may seem awkward at first, but it will work.

Start sewing the outer strip together where there are two layers of fabric. A spiraling effect forms from this point until reaching the end of the strip.

This step forms a tube with pointed edges extending from both ends.

Open the Tube

When the seam is complete, make a press line along one side of the folded tube. Cut the fold off with a ruler and rotary cutter to expose a larger piece of bias/diagonal parallel strips.

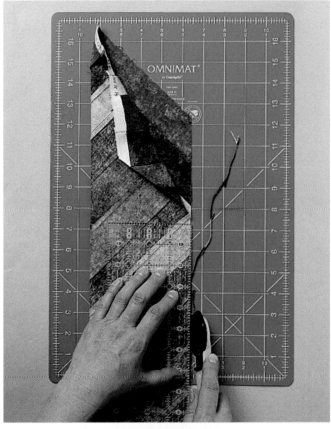

Cutting the Strips

Cut strips of these diagonal pieces, keeping in mind that the 1/4″ seams from each side are removed in the finished piece. As in cutting the original strips, various widths of strips create a unique design. No set size of strips is required for spiraling in the pattern shown here. Therefore, cut several strips in different widths and experiment with them to create a design.

Never cut the whole set until design decisions are made. This allows the opportunity to change your mind and cut wider or narrower strips. Remember that strip piecing offers the opportunity to create as you go. Sometimes the outcome is a total surprise from the original plan.

Throughout the book are designs with definite cut widths or distinct schemes. Choose the idea that most suits the fabrics in your project or experiment to create a new arrangement.

POINT OF INTEREST

- USE A RULER AND ROTARY CUTTER TO CUT THE SPIRALED TUBE OPEN TO MAINTAIN STRAIGHT EDGES.
- CUT SEVERAL SPIRALED STRIPS AT ONCE BEFORE CUTTING THE FULL SET.
- EXPERIMENT AND REPOSITION THE STRIPS BEFORE MAKING FINAL DECISIONS TO COMPLETE THE GARMENT.

Chapter 18

To Match or Not to Match?

Spiraling can offer a variety of opportunities—solid or figured fabrics, wide or narrow strips, gradation combinations rather than contrast. The easiest design is to use a variety of sets with none matching. The overall appearance is quite nice, appearing as though much more effort was involved than actually is.

To Match

To match the sets requires a slightly different approach and a completely different finish. Make two identical sets. The strips must be cut precisely the same width. It's best to have the sewing completed on one machine with seams sewn at the same seam allowance. Because one minor change can prevent the finished piece from matching, it's important to cut and sew precisely. The ends should be squared exactly alike.

Accuracy is of utmost importance! To form a mirror image, place the fabric strips as shown.

Place a pin in the corner, pivot, and sew the strips together as described. Lay the stitched tubes next to each other, making sure each tube spirals in a different direction.

Once the tubes of each set are cut open, it's easy to see how strips cut from the different sets will make a perfect match.

For an even zigzag finish, cut strips the same width from each set. When a hill-and-valley appearance is desired, cut narrow strips from one set and wider strips from the other set. Also consider making an extra set of the wider grouping.

To construct a vest with all matching sets, begin with six identical sets. Remember that each set must be matching. If a coat or a larger size is desired, begin with eight or more sets. These sets should be at least 12″ wide.

Or Not to Match

If the strips don't match once the tubes are stitched and opened, don't worry. The solution is to become a little more creative.

Embroidery beading, corded piping, or other trim can be added between the seams to give the illusion of a matched seam.

Make each seam slightly off to add another designer touch. Who is to judge the original intent?

The brainstorm occurred to me that I could make six identical sets into tubes. Once the tubes were open, I would cut three groups very narrow (1″ to 2″) and the other three groups much wider (3″ to 4″). In the assembling stage, each wide strip would be placed between two narrow strips, resulting in the hill-and-valley effect. As I began to sew these spiraled sets together, it was obvious that the sets would never match because one strip of one set was slightly narrower than the others. Rather than ripping or inserting something, I chose to sew each strip slightly off to give the illusion of a new design. Sometimes designer touches just happen!

It's extremely important that all strips be cut at the same time with the same ruler. The strips should all be sewn on the same machine. You know you will be interrupted as you are sewing. You should have a plan to return to the same tool to complete the project. Otherwise, it will be very difficult to make the sets match in the finished project.

It may seem insignificant to change a tool, needle position, or machine, but any change may require a correction to make the match.

The easiest, most effective place to use matched spiraling is in small areas of a garment such as the shoulder or across the waist. Otherwise, use the unmatched or varied arrangement.

Chapter 19

New Angles

The possibilities of creating with spiraling are endless. For instance, the color combinations can be pastel and very elegant or they could be very bold and bright. Colors could blend together in gradations or they could bounce from light to dark in contrast variations as shown in the two photos below.

The fabric design combinations could include country and calico to plaids and contemporary.

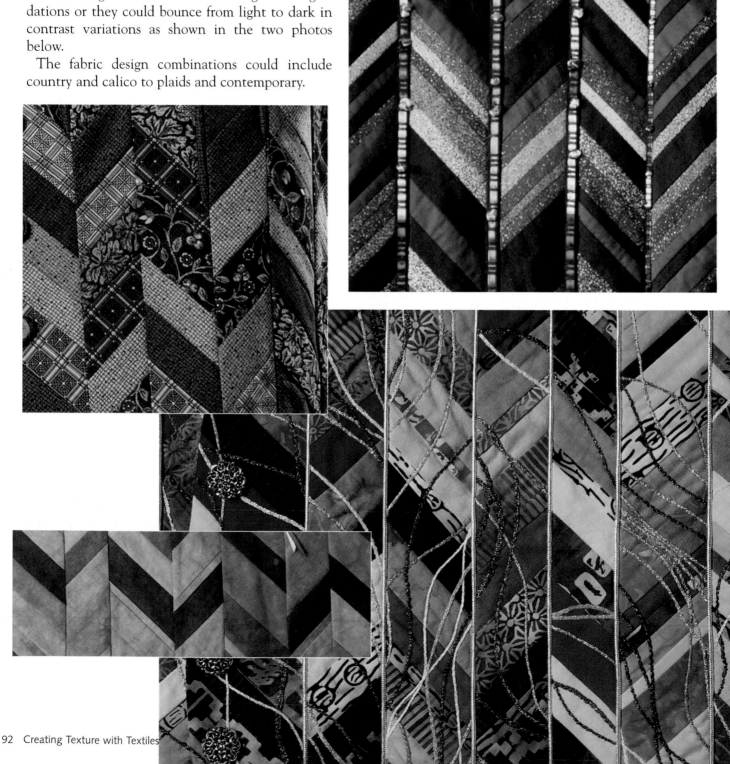

The fabric type could range from basic cotton, handkerchief linen, and wool challis to lamé, velvet, and sueded rayon. Predominantly solid colors can make a rainbow effect or look like a color wheel.

Including stripes on the lengthwise and crosswise grain gives another variety and contrast using the same fabric. From tumbling blocks to herringbone, the range in variation can suit any taste. However, all the angles are 45°.

What about the possibilities of making new angles? It could be so simple. A whole new world of spiraling would open. At first I played with a protractor combined with a ruler. Mathematically, that was the most logical beginning. The plan worked, but there had to be an easier way. Then the brainstorm hit. Mark a ruler with the desired angle and pivot to create that angle on the pieced fabric. This could work!

To Begin

Sew strips together following the traditional spiraling steps. Square the end in the same manner using a see-through ruler.

Make a decision for the angle you wish to make. I like 30° and 22½°. The 30° marking is found on most see-through quilting rulers. Half of 45° is 22½°. These are easy markings to find, however anything in between works fine.

Mark the Ruler

Mark the ruler with the new angle you wish to make. Tape a strip of paper, opaque tape, or the Versa-Guide™ to the ruler at this angle, starting at the corner and angling towards the opposite long side. The paper and tape are makeshift ways to handle the new technique. The Versa-Guide is a polymer sheet with special adhesive on one side designed to use as a guide on the ruler. The thickness acts as a lip for accurate cuts and marks. Place the Versa-Guide on the ruler, beginning at the corner and angling to the desired degree.

New Angles

Rather than use a right angle to form the spiral, pivot the corner until the Versa-Guide matches the long cut strip. Place a pin 1/4″ from the cut edge on the other long side of the ruler.

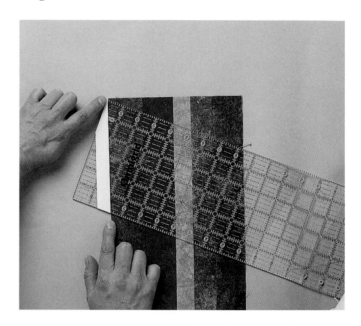

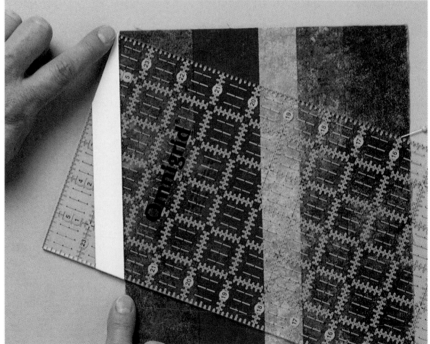

Bring the pivot point to this pin. Begin stitching the spiral at this point and continue stitching the long seam.

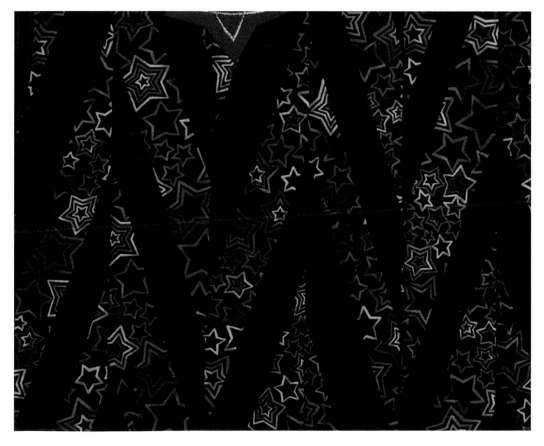

Once the tube is stitched, you'll notice a longer angle forming than the traditional bias. Continue to follow the steps to press and cut open the tube from page 89. The process is the same. The difference is the angle that's formed.

Chapter 20

For Added Length

*T*here are length restrictions with a spiraled set. Generally, the cut strips begin with 45″, the width of the fabric. Depending on the length of the finished project, one set may not be long enough to complete a row on the project. Consider a tunic or full length garment. From a fashion point of view, repeating the same set may be too much repetitious color, too much of a certain design, or too much for a larger size.

Adding a Solid Colored Fabric for Length

Several options extend the length, making the garment a classic, more sophisticated piece rather than an overpowering clash of too much color and print. Consider the basic fabric used in the project. Is it a solid color or print? If it's a print, are the colors bold or subdued? What's the overall feeling for the garment?

Sometimes it may be wise to add a solid color to the bottom of the garment, while other times it may be more appealing to add one of the darker printed fabrics.

Make the garment pleasant to the eye. More attention should be drawn closer to the face, keeping the predominant colors and design in the shoulder and neck area. Corded piping or other trim in this area

calls attention to the top of the garment. As the garment progresses toward the bottom, the design should darken, taking the viewing eye from the bottom of the garment to the top where most of the design is.

Seam Extension

To use one fabric to extend the length of the garment, cut the added fabric at a 45° angle, using the guidelines on a ruler. This is the same angle as the spiraled fabric.

Place right sides together with the point extended so that the intersection of the two pieces is equal to the seam allowance.

Stitch this seam and press towards the darker fabric.

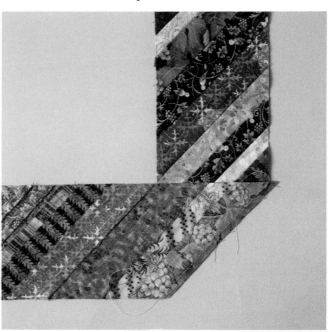

Adding a Spiraled Section

For other garments or projects, the overall appeal may require a continued spiral section. Make several additional spiraled sets with the darker colors from the upper sets or a new set of darker colors. These spiraled strips in the sets for the lower edge of a garment may be wider than the strips used in the upper portion of the garment.

Wide Fill Piecing

Black 100% cotton and black polished fabric create the illusion of two tones in the continuation of the "Pointillist Palette" fabric. Several black fabrics from different manufacturers could make the same shading illusion.

Narrow Strip Piecing with Darker Shades

Predominant green and gold with very little purple were spiraled in the upper portion of "I Heard It Through the Grapevine" fabric. Mostly shades of purple were spiraled for the extension into the tunic length vest.

Embroidered Beading for More Detail

Embroidered beading with gold edge trim ribbon adds variety in the upper portion of the garment where more variety is needed with darker fabrics. The darker groupings without the embroidery and gold add darker shades to the bottom.

Continue the length of the garment according to its style and design. Choose a solid or figured darker fabric to fill in a small area. Continue a longer version with a spiraled piece. The options vary from garment to garment. Experiment, create, enjoy!

POINT OF INTEREST

➛ADDING LENGTH TO CONVENTIONAL SPIRALING IS LIKE COMBINING TWO BIAS STRIPS TOGETHER, EXCEPT THE PIECES ARE WIDER.

➛THE OPTIONS FOR ADDING LENGTH ARE VARIED.

CONSIDER THESE IDEAS AND THE PROSPECT FOR OTHERS BEGINS TO ARISE. ONE THING ALWAYS LEADS TO ANOTHER.

Chapter 21
Putting It All Together

*B*ecause the cut strips are on the bias, a foundation or base is necessary to maintain the shape of the garment. Several fabrics and battings are suitable for this project, however, the desired finished weight will determine which to use.

The Backing

Lightweight cotton, flannel, muslin, garment batting, or fabric from the stockpile that will never be used (make sure the color will not bleed or show through) make a good base and do not add too much weight to the garment.

Fairfield, Hobbs, Mountain Mist, Morning Glory, and Warm & Natural make a variety of battings that can be incorporated into a garment. The heavier or loftier batting may require a slightly larger size in the pattern to accommodate the extra bulk in the garment. Usually, going up half to one size is sufficient fabric to avoid making the garment too small.

Ghee's Shirt Tail Vest Pattern #595 is used to illustrate this technique, although any pattern could be used with this construction procedure.

Marking the Base

This system is much like the quilt-as-you-go method or stitch and flip. Always cut the base larger than necessary for the finished project. With a removable marking pencil, mark the outline of the pattern directly on the base to use as a guide. When the base is a woven, be certain the outline of the pattern is on grain. Mark several other lines parallel to grain at 2″ to 3″ intervals to assist in the stitching.

Begin at the Center

Generally it's advisable to begin in the center of a project and work out. However, this may vary from project to project. On a garment back, begin on the center back. On the front, begin at the center front, though the front has a cut edge and the back has a fold.

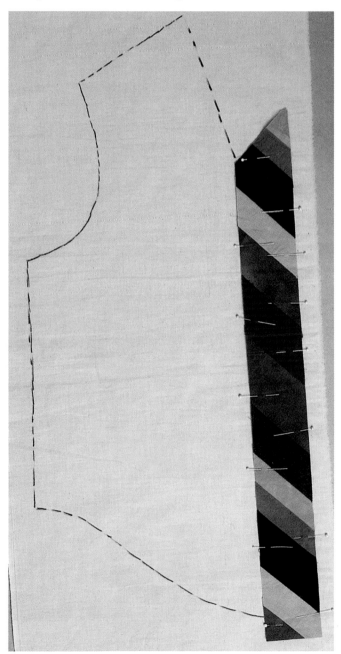

Place the first piece along a straight grain at the center, right side up. Pin at intervals with the pin perpendicular or right angle to the cut edge to hold the placement and prevent slippage. With right sides together, place the second piece, matching a cut edge.

the pattern as a cutting guide rather than the drawn outline, since it's possible for the base to shift with many seams. Baste 1/8″ inside the marking.

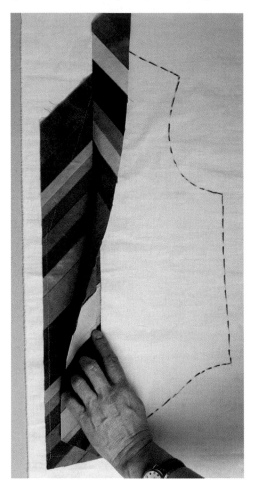

Adding Other Strips

Open the piece to expose the right sides and continue in the same manner. Add the next piece, right sides together; stitch and open to expose the right sides. Because there is an outline guide on the base for the finished project, it's easy to judge where the next piece will be placed.

It's very easy for the bias strips used to make spiraling to stretch while handling. This will cause the lines to become uneven in places. Double check your work to be certain each flipped strip is straight before continuing with the next strip. It's easier to double check before you sew than to rip several rows when you discover the strips are getting crooked.

Continue to add pieces until the pattern shape markings drawn on the base are completely covered. Use

POINT OF INTEREST

- WARMER CLIMATES NEED LIGHTER BACKING, WHILE COOLER REGIONS REQUIRE HEAVIER BATTING. USE THE FOUNDATION SUITABLE FOR THE END USE OF THE GARMENT OR PROJECT.
- ENLARGE THE PATTERN A HALF SIZE WHEN USING HEAVIER BATTING.
- KEEP THE QUILT-AS-YOU-GO LINES STRAIGHT TO AVOID SHIFTING INTO CROOKED PIECING.

Chapter 22

The Finishing Touch with...

To transform a garment into a fashion statement rather than just a vest, consider several elements. My preference is to add dimension and definition to the vertical or horizontal seams between elements of embellishment or piecing and other design work. Sometimes this addition is the complete length of the seam, while in other cases it may cover a portion of the seam. This is determined by the finished design desired. I always complete a garment with a detail that adds character.

Piping

Piping is simply a narrow strip of folded fabric inserted into a seam with a small edge remaining visible. Normally, this strip of fabric should be cut on the bias to accommodate curves and corners. However, because the placement on the spiraled garment is always straight, I sometimes cheat and cut my pieces crossgrain on the fabric. The crossgrain has a slight stretch, making it more suitable for piping than the length grain. When using a stripe or plaid, I generally cut on the bias. I sometimes use crossgrain on strips. It depends. It never fails, whenever I make a rule, I always break it. Make your choice.

For piping, cut strips 1″ wide. Fold and press the strips with wrong sides together, making the strip 1/2″. Place the cut edge of piping even with the cut edge of the spiraled strip. Apply the next strip with right sides together, encasing the piping between the two layers of strips. When using 1/4″ seam allowances, the piping is exposed 1/4″ when the strips are turned. If a slightly wider or narrower piece of piping is preferred, change the needle position from left or right to accommodate the desired finished width of piping. It doesn't matter if the seam allowance is generous or a skimpy 1/4″ as long as the raw edge is secure.

Piping a Yoke

Rather than continue the piping the full length of the garment, consider using piping on just part of the length. One of the best guidelines is to incorporate the piping in an area similar to the area of a yoke.

To finish the piping in a yoke area of a spiraled garment, curve the piping into the seam allowance at the point where the end is desired.

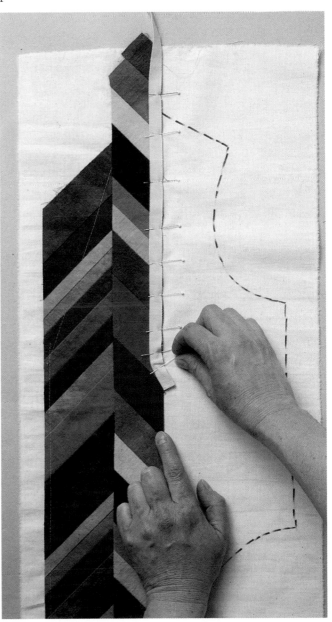

After stitching the seam, trim the excess piping. All rows of piping need not end at the same level of the garment. Actually, the best finish is to end at obviously different levels.

POINT OF INTEREST

- FOR A WIDER PIPING, VARY THE WIDTH OF THE CUT STRIP. CONSIDER THE POSITION ON THE GARMENT TO AVOID MAKING THE STRIP TOO WIDE.
- CONSIDER THE CROSSGRAIN TO SAVE FABRIC FOR PIPING-TRIM IN STRAIGHT AREAS.
- USE BIAS PIPING TO TURN CURVES.
- STRIPS OFFER THE OPTION OF BIAS OR CROSSGRAIN. THIS IS A DESIGN DILEMMA.

Continuous Bias

CONTINUOUS BIAS: CONTINUING WITHOUT A BREAK. AN UNBROKEN OR UNCUT STRIP OF FABRIC CUT ON THE DIAGONAL OR BIAS GRAIN OF FABRIC.

A great number of my designs have an area separated by or completely surrounded with corded piping. I can use yards of corded piping before I realize it. It's both easier and more practical to make one continuous strip rather than constantly cutting and sewing several narrow strips together. This continuous strip technique is one I learned many years ago in my home economics class. It's possible to make approximately 12 yards of 1¼″ bias from 1/2 yard of fabric.

Cutting the Triangles

To begin, cut two bias triangles from opposite corners of the fabric.

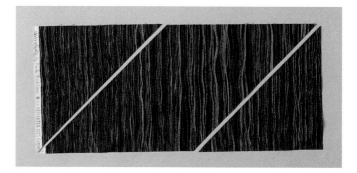

From a bias edge, make a cut 1¼″ wide by approximately 6″ long, leaving the cut piece attached.

Fold the straight grain edges together to form a tube. Allow the 1¼″ strip to fall free. Be certain to place the straight edges together so that the seam allowance is straight.

Stagger the point by 1/4″, the width of the seam allowance. Stitch to form a spiral seam on the tube. Press the seam open.

Begin cutting, following the determined width, to produce yards of continuous bias.

↪ADJUST THE WIDTH OF THE CUT STRIP TO ALTER THE WIDTH OF A CONTINUOUS BIAS. CONTINUE WITH OTHER STEPS.

↪IT'S VERY EASY TO USE YARDS OF CORDED PIPING IN A GARMENT. SOME OF THE GARMENTS I'VE MADE USE AS MANY AS 20 YARDS.

Corded Piping

Corded piping is a narrow strip of bias fabric containing a cord. Many times a purchased decorative corded piping is available to enhance the design.

The purchased corded piping is available in basic fabric or decorative patterns by the yard or in small packages. However, other times you'll need to make fabric corded piping to match or contrast.

Traditionally, bias is used for corded piping. Always use bias with a stripe or plaid. However, because fabric gives on the crosswise grain, it's permissible to use the crosswise grain when trimming straight seams like the vertical seams of spiraling.

Different sizes of cord will require different amounts of fabric. For small to medium corded piping, the bias strips should be 1¼˝ wide. This technique is made easier by using one of the feet designed specifically for this purpose. Position the cording in the center of the fabric strip. Fold the fabric in half over the cord.

Keeping the cut edges together, place the cording under the ridge or tunnel in the foot.

For very small cording, use the largest pintucking foot. Change the needle position to stitch close to the cording but do not stitch too close. When making corded piping, the bias fabric will eventually be stitched three times. Each stitching will be closer to the cording, making the final stitching the closest. Moving the needle position for this purpose is ideal to avoid showing the previous rows of stitching.

Just as in the piping, the corded piping may not need to extend the full length of the garment. The corded piping will curve into the seam allowance just as the piping. Too much corded piping at the seam intersections will cause extra bulk, which you can eliminate by pulling and trimming the cording from the seam allowance where the corded piping curves into the seam allowance. After trimming, run your finger over the corded piping to relax the cord.

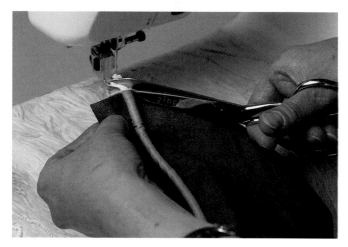

Continuous Corded Piping

Most of my corded piping continues to the end of a seam. However, I like to place a continuous piece completely around areas, such as around the outside edge of a jacket or the edge of sleeves.

Choose an inconspicuous place to begin, such as the center back. Leave a 1˝ tail at the beginning. Stitch around the area and return to the beginning. Curve the 1˝ tail towards the outside cut edge. Overlap the bias cording slightly and curve towards the cut edge.

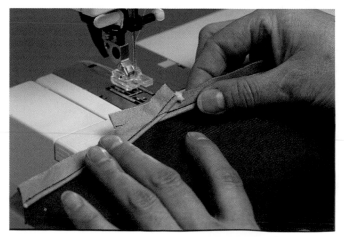

Removing Bulk

Too much corded piping at the seam intersections will cause extra bulk. To eliminate the bulk, pull and trim the cording from the seam allowance as before. Any overlapping seams will become less bulky to sew. The end result is more attractive.

Variety with Double Corded Piping

For variety with corded piping, construct double corded piping using different colors of fabrics and different sizes of cording. Add a stripe or plaid. Combine textured braid with other solids or figured corded piping. In other words, experiment.

To make double corded piping, allow a wider seam allowance on the continuous bias. Place one layer of corded piping—usually the smaller one—on top, butting the cord together. Stitch with the piping foot to hold the two together and continue with the regular seaming process. The smaller cord will be closer to the seam.

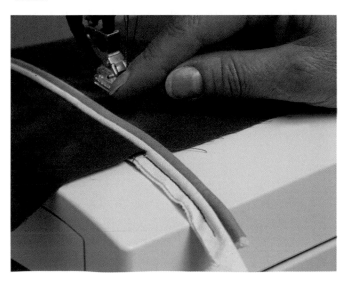

↪CONSIDER USING SEVERAL SIZES OF PIPING IN ONE GARMENT TO ADD VARIETY.
↪USE CORDED PIPING ONLY IN THE SEAMS WHICH CROSS THE SHOULDER. IT'S NOT NECESSARY TO USE CORDED PIPING IN THE SEAMS UNDER THE ARM.
↪USE A DOUBLE LAYER OF FABRIC ON COARSELY TWISTED CORDING TO PREVENT THE RIDGES FROM SHOWING THROUGH.

Embroidered Beading

Another option in joining sections of embellishment while maintaining definition between the different rows of spiraling is to use embroidered beading.

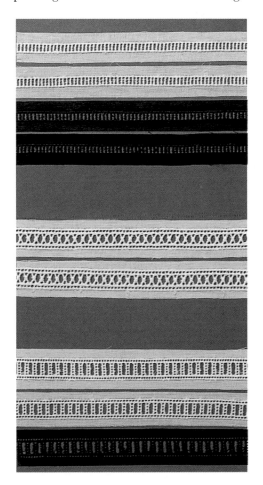

This type of beading is basically a batiste with embroidery stitching to form slits through which ribbon can be laced. I like to use embroidery beading when additional color is necessary to complete the look I need for a garment.

Embroidery Beading without Seam Allowances

The extra batiste on the edges of the beading is trimmed away. Align the edgestitching foot with the embroidery. Adjust the zigzag on the machine so that the zig goes into the hole of the embroidery and the zag goes over the edge. Use this process when the piecing is finished and more detail is desired on the garment. The embroidery will lay on

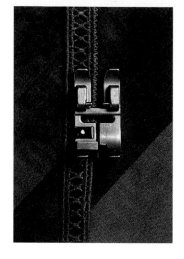

top of the piecing. It won't join elements together, simply overlap them.

Embroidery Beading with Seam Allowances

There's another option with embroidery to combine bulky sections of embellishment. This technique works best with straight seams because the width of the beading does not curve well. This is another use for the edgestitching foot.

With the beading on top, right sides together, match the cut edge of the batiste with the cut edge of the garment. Align the bar of the edgestitching foot to the right ridge of the beading. This will act as a guide, making the stitching position accurate.

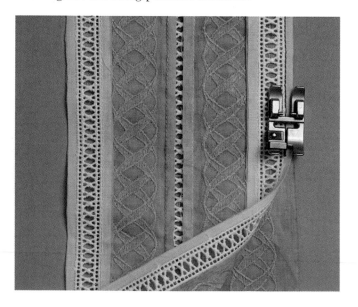

Move the needle position to the right and stitch approximately 1/16″ from the ridge. The small distance between the last ridge of beading and stitching allows the beading to turn. Known as the turn of the fabric, this technique helps maintain a flat seam.

With either of these techniques, the bar of the edgestitching foot acts as a guide for accuracy. All beading will be exposed to the maximum and little bulk remains in the seam allowance.

The original design for beading was to guide ribbon evenly through the holes to emphasize extra color. The weaving may be irregular with occasional knots for added design. There's no rule stating that the weaving pattern must be symmetrical. Even if there is a rule, now's the time to break it! Guide the ribbon with a tapestry needle under some of the slits and over others. Don't establish a balanced design. Go over one, under three, over two, under five, or whatever strikes your fancy. Remember, it's okay to break the rules. Every once in a while, tie a knot.

Allow the design and color of the ribbon to add dimension. Use two layers of ribbon through the same slits. When the knot is tied, the colors will flip, making a two-toned section. The variety of colors in the ribbon will add spark to the garment. Small tricks like this add designer touches, creating one-of-a-kind results. Make a mistake once in a while. The mistake may lead to a better arrangement than the original plan!

- WEAVE TWO RIBBONS THROUGH THE SLITS OF EMBROIDERY RATHER THAN ONE. TIE A KNOT OCCASIONALLY TO CHANGE THE COLOR AND ADD VARIETY.
- EMBROIDERED BEADING IS AVAILABLE IN WHITE, ECRU, AND BLACK. USE THE SPRAY ON TUMBLE DYES TO ADD COLOR TO MATCH THE GARMENT.
- EMBROIDERY TRIMS THAT ARE 10 TO 15 YARDS LONG ARE MADE ON MACHINES. THE SEAM ALLOWANCE FOUND ON THE BOLT OF TRIM IS JOINING EACH PIECE TOGETHER. THIS IS NOT A FLAW.
- TO COMBINE PIECES OF EMBROIDERY BEADING TOGETHER, OVERLAP TWO HOLES AND INSERT AS IF THEY WERE ONE PIECE. ONCE THE RIBBONS ARE WOVEN, NO ONE CAN FIND THE MEND.
- DETERMINE THE BEST METHOD FOR ATTACHING EMBROIDERY BEADING TO A GARMENT. TRIM THE BATISTE FOR A FLAT FINISH. USE THE SEAM ALLOWANCE WHEN ADDING BULKY PINTUCKING, CRINKLING, OR PIECING.

Inserting a Strip

Occasionally a problem arises because there are too few large pieces of fabric for a garment. Because there wasn't enough fabric, the lining was pieced with the leftover fabrics. A puzzle was drawn on the lining. To join the pieces, a strip of fabric along the selvage including the designer's name was incorporated between the sections.

Sometimes there is space to include a 1/4″ seam allowance. At other times, the seams must be over-lapped and stitched with a decorative stitch. In this case, a maximum width stretch stitch, combined with a satin stitch, was used on the selvage and 1/4″ seam allowance on the cut side. Contrasting thread in the bobbin with the tensions tightened made a special design.

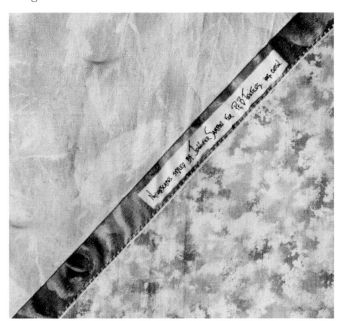

Gathered Corded Piping

The making of gathered corded piping begins like traditional corded piping. Though a bias strip is desired for stripes and plaids, the crossgrain can be used when the fabric is minimal. Because many gathers are included with the piping, the cording easily rounds curves and corners.

Using a slightly wider strip of cording makes the gathers and seam allowances easier to work with. Fold the strip in half over the cording. Stitch with the piping foot, using the far right needle position. This stitching will appear approximately 1/8″ to 1/16″ from the cord, allowing the cord to slip freely through the bias.

Before gathering the piping with the cording, mark the garment sections in quarters or eighths. Decide how much fullness you want in the cording. Usually 1½ times to 2 times is enough. Then mark the corded piping accordingly.

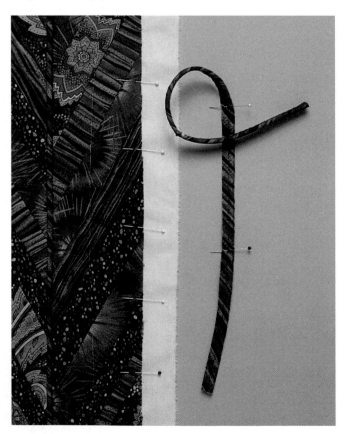

Pull the cording to form gathers on the piping, matching the corresponding marks on the garment. Evenly distribute the gathers between the marks.

Stitch the gathered corded piping to the garment with the needle position closer to the corded piping. Continue to add the next garment section to the corded piping.

This type of corded piping is particularly nice around pintucks, heirloom sewing, and any area that's not crinkled. The gathered corded piping sometimes loses its identity when placed next to wrinkled fabric, though you may consider it an option.

From Cord to Corded Piping

Occasionally I discover a wonderful cord and wish it were a corded piping. Some of these cords could be couched, but the zigzag would overpower the cord, taking away from the design. I discovered that it's very easy to create a corded piping from a cord by adding a lip to the cord. Seams Great® (a sheer seam finishing product) is light enough to form the lip of the piping without adding extra bulk.

➤WHEN WORKING WITH CURVED EDGES, DON'T STRETCH THE BIAS STRIP OR THE FABRIC WILL DISTORT AND SHRINK WITH THE FIRST WASHING.

➤PIPING, THE VARIOUS TYPES OF CORDED PIPING, AND EMBROIDERY BEADING ARE THE FINAL ADDITIONS TO ANY GARMENT TO COMPLETE THE ELEMENT OF TEXTURE. BE SURE TO USE THE FINISH THAT ADDS THE RIGHT DESIGNER TOUCH.

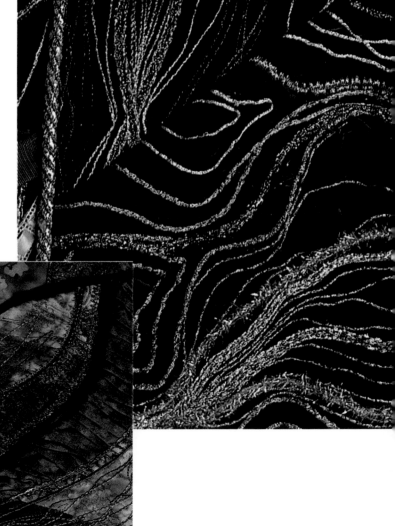

Fold the Seams Great or other sheer bias strip in half and press. Align the cord under the groove in the piping foot and position the folded edge of the sheer bias next to the cord.

Using a blanket stitch, stitch the two pieces together. It may be necessary to adjust the stitch width to grab more or less of the cord. The needle should stitch several straight stitches in the sheer and one zigzag in the cord. Be sure to keep the sheer next to the cord so the two pieces align with each other.

Cheryl Phillips

Chapter 23
Combining the Elements

COMBINING THE ELEMENTS:
TO JOIN OR BE JOINED
INTO A GROUP. USING A
NUMBER OF PARTS TO
MAKE A WHOLE.

*T*he easiest way to avoid sizing problems when texturing or making special effects with fabric is to always make more than necessary. It's simple to cut down a piece to the size required, yet very disappointing to come up short. No matter which is the case, whether trimming down, adding more to size up, or using leftovers to build another project, use something to separate the sections, to give each segment its own framework without dominating the entire piece.

Corded piping segregates the different segments or designs yet gives each area definition and dimension.

Each portion has its own border before another technique begins. For variety and color, use double or triple corded piping.

Perhaps embroidery beading works better with highlights from additional ribbon color.

Remember that the boundary around each element should accent or outline the work rather than overpower the composition.

In the Beginning

In this sample, there are two techniques. One is spiraling and the other couching with decorative stitching. The easiest format to follow is to make one side pieced and the other couched. Cut the pieces in half and stitch opposite pieces together. It sounds simple and it is. There are a few tips to make it easier.

The Piecing Side

Trace the outline of the pattern on the base before piecing. Rather than mark the lower curved edge of the hem, extend the piecing straight down approximately 3″. Because there's an outline guide for the finished project, it's easy to judge where the next piece will be placed. Continue to add pieces until the pattern shape markings are completely covered.

The Couching Side

Be certain to flip the front pattern piece over to insure a left and right front. Trace the pattern on the crinkled fabric 1″ larger than the needed size to allow for shrinkage with stitching. Again, make the pattern tracing straight down and longer to allow for seam allowances and flip flopping the pattern. It's easier to stitch long decorative lines than to work with short squatty pieces of fabric. The lines can be smooth and flowing.

Cutting the Pieces

After completing the embellishment on both front pieces, you must decide where to cut. I personally don't like a horizontal line going completely across my body in the waist area. It draws attention to my midsection which isn't the most flattering portion of my body. However, I don't mind a line coming from the side and stopping at the center. To make four sections on the front of a garment, the most flattering design is four unequal sections. My favorite horizontal lines are either above or below the bust point and just above or below the waistline, depending on the length of the garment.

Decide where the line should be drawn on the left side. Allow 1″ for the shoulder and section seam allowances—that is 1/4″ seam allowances and a little play. Cut at this point.

Make a decision where the line should be drawn on the left side. Again, allow 1″ for the shoulder and section seam allowances. Using a ruler and rotary cutter, cut a straight horizontal line across the embellished piece.

Cut on the Grain Line

Be sure the grain lines are accurate. It will be obvious on the pieced side. Use the vertical stitch and flip lines as a guide. Use the pattern grain line to make the decision on the crinkled side. Fold the pattern at the appropriate horizontal position, being certain the grain line overlaps itself.

Swapping the Pieces

Sew the lower section of the right side to the upper portion of the left side.

Choose a finishing touch to complement the two sections. Refer to the Finishing Touch Chapter for guides and suggestions. There are no set rules. Study the fabric colors and prints, style of the garment, and general overall appeal to determine what to use between the sections. Sometimes it may be as simple as placing a trim on top of the seam allowance.

Sew the lower section of the left side to the upper portion of the right side, using the same guidelines.

Cutting the Pattern

After the sections are sewn together, place the pattern on top, paying attention to shoulder, neck, armscye, and hemline. This is the last opportunity to make adjustments before cutting the garment. Check the grain line and cut. Be certain to flip the pattern piece over before cutting the other side. The armscye and neck area are very similar at this point in construction.

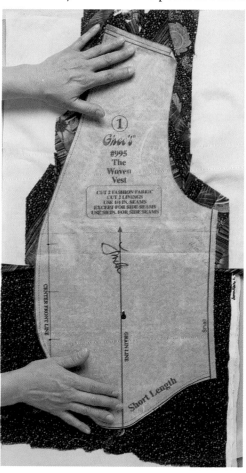

➤MOST STITCHERS I KNOW ATTEMPT TO BUILD SOMETHING FROM A CORE. I FIND IT EASIER TO MAKE LARGER PIECES AND CUT TO SIZE.

➤WITH EMBELLISHING AND PIECING, IT'S DIFFICULT TO KNOW THE FINISHED SIZE BEFOREHAND. SOMETIMES THE PIECES EXPAND, OTHER TIMES THEY REDUCE MORE THAN EXPECTED. IT'S EASIER TO PLAN AFTER KNOWING THE FINISHED SIZE OF THOSE COMPLETED PARTS.

➤DOUBLE CHECK TO SEE THAT A LEFT AND RIGHT SIDE ARE CUT. FLIP THE PATTERN PIECE OVER TO ACCOMPLISH THIS. ALWAYS DOUBLE CHECK TO AVOID CUTTING TWO OF THE SAME SIDE.

➤ALWAYS INSERT SOMETHING BETWEEN FORMS OF EMBELLISHMENT TO DEFINE EACH SECTION.

➤PIPING, CORDED PIPING, AND DOUBLE CORDED PIPING ADD VERY SUBTLE DETAIL.

➤EMBROIDERY BEADING OFFERS THE LAST OPPORTUNITY FOR ADDITIONAL COLOR TO TIE THE SECTIONS TOGETHER.

Chapter 24

Uneven Edges

Variety is the spice of life. Sometimes it's fun to complete a garment with an unusual finish. Why always have a straight or traditional lower edge? The shirt tail is a nice finish. But spiraling forms its own uneven edge. Why not let the bottom be determined by the design of the pieced garment?

Stitch the Hemline

Fully line the garment, leaving the bottom edge completely open. The lining should be as long as the garment. Hang the garment on a hanger overnight to let the fabric fall to a relaxed position. Pin the layers of piecing, backing, and lining together with pins vertical to the hemline. Using the desired finish color of thread in the bobbin as well as the top, stitch these layers together with a small straight stitch along the desired finished length. There should be at least 1/4″ waste along the edge to avoid stretching the piecing. This technique doesn't require a hem. The straight stitching will be the finished length. Nothing will be added and nothing taken away.

Trim to the Hemline

Very carefully trim to this stitching. There should be no more than 1/16″ fabric remaining between the stitching and the cut edge. Use the point of the scissors to make clean straight corners.

Stabilize the Hemline

Zigzag over the gimpe or a lightweight cord with a stitch width of 1½ to 2 and length of 1½. The center hole of the multi-hole cording foot or the single hole cording foot keeps the gimpe perfectly aligned. An open toe appliqué foot could be used for this purpose, however, use caution to keep the cord straight and center. The purpose of this stitching is to stabilize the finished edge with gimpe to avoid stretching with wear. Using a satin stitch at this point causes a ripple. Making the prettiest finish requires stitching three times.

Final Stitching

The final stitching is the most important. It covers the other stitching and gimpe, adds weight, and produces a rolled finished edge. Adjust the stitch width slightly wider than the previous zigzag to make sure the first stitching is covered. Adjust the stitch length to the perfect satin. This means the stitches lay side-by-side. Don't overlap or allow space between them. With the open toe appliqué foot, stitch the final round over all the previous stitches. The needle will go in the fabric to the left and into open air on the right, causing the thread to overlap the edge with a smooth finish.

It may be necessary to help the fabric along the corners since the feed dogs have nothing to hold to on the right side. Don't rush at this point, it takes time for the machine to complete the stitching. Don't push the fabric. If the rolled finish isn't filled in sufficiently, make a fourth round. Be certain the stitch width is slightly wider than previously sewn for the best finish.

POINT OF INTEREST

- USE THE SAME COLOR AND TYPE OF THREAD ON TOP AND IN THE BOBBIN.
- A DECORATIVE THREAD SUCH AS RAYON OR METALLIC MAKES AN ARTISTIC FINISH.
- IT MAY BE NECESSARY TO TIGHTEN THE TENSION SLIGHTLY FOR SMOOTHER COVERAGE.

- WHEN A BIT OF THE BACKING OR FABRIC SHOWS THROUGH THE ROLLED STITCHING, COLOR IT WITH A PERMANENT MARKER THE COLOR OF THE STITCHING.
- IT REQUIRES TIME TO COMPLETE THE FINAL STITCHING OF THE UNEVEN EDGE. GO SLOW, IT'S WORTH THE EFFORT.

Chapter 25
Estimating Yardage for Spiraling

Determining the amount of fabric can be tricky. Whenever I try to purchase the exact amount of fabric for a project, I usually regret doing so because more often than not I wind up a little short. It's really best to purchase a little more than you'll need. The little bit of extra money is well spent to avoid the aches and pains and lost time involved in solving the problem caused by being a "little short."

Originally I planned to include a yardage chart to help you calculate yardage for different size projects. After constructing many samples using a variety of fabrics, I found it impossible to give exact yardage for any projects. There are too many variables. I purchase fabrics differently for piecing projects than whole garments. My philosophy is to adapt basic techniques to the fabrics chosen for the project. When I considered that fabrics similar to the ones used in this book may not be available and all the other variables, I abandoned my plan to give you a yardage chart. I know you will understand once you start cutting and sewing the sets.

The easiest calculation is to have the total of all yardage combined equal the necessary yardage to make that garment. For instance, if the garment requires 1½ yards to complete and there are six fabrics used, 1/4 yard of each fabric is necessary. The spark or filler color may require more fabric, while the other colors may require less. Some fabrics, perhaps leftovers from another project, may have one or two strips. This amount is hardly enough to consider in yardage. But leftovers of several different strips begin to add up as the process continues. Piping, corded piping, tucks, and other detail procedures use fabric too. It never hurts to have more fabric than necessary.

Consider the following guidelines to work with most sizes. Add another set or two for larger sizes:

- Four sets 16″ wide make a short length (just below the waistline) vest for most sizes front and back.

- Allow six sets, with two of the sets in darker shades, for tunic length.

- Allow eight sets, with four of the sets in darker shades, for duster length.

- Two narrow sets 10″ to 12″ wide make a partial garment front or one side of the garment in all sizes.

- A garment with the tumbling block method uses four darker and two lighter sets, each 12″ to 16″ wide. Allow more sets for longer length.

- Herringbone spiraling uses equal amounts of two fabrics. One fabric could be a bold geometric print with the other fabric a solid.

- Spiraling a large print generally uses equal amounts of that print fabric and one solid color fabric.

- Purchase two yards of a stripe or gradation fabrics. This allows 45″ to cut lengthwise and 3/4 yard to cut crosswise.

- Very narrow strips use more fabric than imaginable. Allow extra.

- When in doubt, always purchase more. I usually purchase no less than one yard of any given fabric. If I really like it, I purchase two yards. If there's a possibility that it could be used for lining too, I purchase three yards.

- Buy fabric. It's fun!

Chapter 26

A Small Project with Leftovers

Save all leftovers from various sewing projects for future use. They make it easier to design a handbag or belt for each unique creation, the beginning of another garment, or a gift for a sewing friend. Treat leftovers in the sewing room like leftovers in the kitchen. Add a little something and create something new.

An eyeglass case is a very simple project to use up some of those tidbits. It can double as a holder for the rotary cutter, pencils, portable telephone, or personal products. It can be shortened for a coin purse, jewelry case, credit cards, a garage for toy cars, or Grandma's brag book. It can be lengthened for the curling iron or knitting needles. This is a wonderful non-gender, every-age idea for presents made personally by you.

Begin with Fabric Lining, Fleece, and Leftover Fabrics

To make this project you need a fabric lining and fleece 10˝ by the desired length plus 1½˝. The lining will show in the finished case. Place the wrong side of the lining on the fleece, matching all edges. Place a strip of piecing right side up on the other side of the fleece. Don't center this first piecing because it will cause bulk in the finished bottom seam. There are times when it's best not to match!

Begin the Stitch and Flip

Place another strip of piecing right sides together, matching cut edges. Begin stitching in the same manner as "Putting It All Together," or stitch and flip. The difference here is that there's lining on the back side. The stitching will incorporate piecing, fleece, and lining with the stitching showing on the lining side.

Add another strip of piecing to complete the stitch and flip. This piecing, once stitched and flipped, should cover the entire fleece.

Corded Piping for Detail

Corded piping is placed on the lining side top edge with cut edges together. Logically this seems backwards. In the finished eyeglass case, the corded piping will be flipped to the front. Stitch with a piping foot or three-groove pintuck foot, depending on the size of the corded piping.

Form the Casing

To form the casing for the metal eyeglass frame, fold the right sides of the fashion fabric together 1˝ from the cut edge.

Tuck under the seam allowance and stitch in the ditch along the corded piping to hold the seam allowance under. Another alternative is edgestitching.

Fold the casing in half lengthwise, with right sides together. Insert the frame from each open end with curves facing each other.

Push the frames in as snug as possible and pin to hold them tightly in place. Stitch down the side seam and across the bottom. Be certain the beginning stitches by the frame are secured. This is the area of the finished case that will have the most wear.

Complete the Case

Turn the fashion fabric (piecing) right side out to complete the eyeglass case. This is a very quick simple project and it helps to use up those valuable leftovers.

Sometimes the leftovers are better or more fun to work with than the original piece! They have had time to mellow and blend—to mix into a new entity.

POINT OF INTEREST

↝ USE GATHERED LACE OR A RUFFLE RATHER THAN CORDED PIPING TO FINISH THE UPPER EDGE WHERE SUITABLE. AS A SERGER PROJECT, USE THE NARROW ROLLED EDGE TO MAKE THE CORDED PIPING.

↝ BE CERTAIN THE FOLD DOWN IS LARGE ENOUGH TO SLIDE THE METAL FRAME THROUGH.

↝ THOUGH THESE INSTRUCTIONS ARE FOR THE SEWING MACHINE, THE SERGER COULD EASILY FINISH THE EDGES.

↝ BEGIN WITH DOUBLE-FACED QUILTED FABRIC AND EMBROIDER A SIMPLE DESIGN.

↝ USE LEFTOVERS OF HEIRLOOM LACES, PINTUCKING, DECORATIVE STITCHING, AS WELL AS PIECING TO CREATE UNIQUE DESIGNS.

About the Author

Designer Linda McGehee has a diverse background with 40 years experience. From garments to handbags, from piecing to heirloom, from surface manipulation of fabric to combining methods and techniques, Linda has been involved. She has written award-winning books about the techniques she has learned and mastered. In addition, Linda has traveled the globe to demonstrate her skills and lecture from her books to audiences that include trade and machine conventions, consumers, guilds, shops, and television viewers. She also produces "Ghee's Sewing Escapes" annually.

She has authored and published several books on sewing: *Texture with Textiles* (winner of PCM's 1992 Product of Excellence award in the sewing book division), *More Texture with Textiles* (finalist for the same award in 1993), and *A Companion Project Book, Spiraling Schemes and Chromatics* (winner of PRIMEDIA's 1997 Product of Excellence award in the sewing book division).

Linda has designed and created garments for the prestigious Fairfield Fashion Show, Statements, Capitol Imports, and *Better Homes & Gardens*. These garments are works of art combining many of the techniques from her books. "On My Way to the Mardi Gras" from the Fairfield 1996-1997 show graced the October 1996 cover of *Craft & Needlework Age Magazine*.

Linda is the owner of Ghee's mail order sewing and notions company. The most popular patterns are her designs for handbags with ready-to-wear handbag hardware. For information about Linda's international mail order service and schedule of seminars, contact Ghee's, 2620 Centenary #2-250, Shreveport, LA 71104. Voice: (318) 226-1701, fax: (318) 226-1781, e-mail: ghees@softdisk.com, web: http//www.ghees.com.

Gallery

"The Bag Lady Goes to Mardi Gras" (left) graced the runway of the 1994-1995 Fairfield Show. Yards and yards of threads and yarns couched over the crinkled cotton velvet from Capitol Imports. Rows of Tumble Dyed embroidery trims in Mardi Gras colors of purple, gold, and green created the lattice piecing. Handmade buttons by Albe Creations add a finishing touch to the pintucked collar. This garment was created in a mere 200 hours.

Photographer Frank Reimer

"On My Way to the Mardi Gras" (above) was created for the prestigious Diamond Intrigue 1996-1997 Fairfield Fashion Show. Vivid solids from Dyenamics Hand Dyed Fabrics combined with Balis from Hoffman California Fabrics began the base of this anything but basic suit. Glitter embellished the spiraling by couching heavier threads over the piecing. Over 87 spools of thread were stitched into couching, decorative stitching, and decorative pintucks.

Photographer Brad Stanton

Designed for Statements, an invitational show debuting at the Portland Quilt Market, "Mixed Media" combines couching, lattice piecing, pintucks, and heirloom on the base of the Folkwear Hungarian Szür Pattern. Nature Scapes by P & B Fabrics, Kreinik braids and ribbons, and Capitol Imports embroidery trims combine to make this dazzling combination.

Over 100 yards of lace and embroidery were used in this basic jacket. Crinkling, pintucking, couching, heirloom, and corded piping were applied to handkerchief linen to complete "I'd Rather Wear Lace." This jacket has over ten spools of thread in addition to an investment of 100 hours of sewing for a true heirloom.

My favorite techniques incorporated into handbags.

Never let anything go to waste. This vest was created using the leftover spiraling piecework from my Fairfield garment.

Lattice piecing created in subdued coloration. Elegant with ruffled ribbon, decorative stitching, flat ribbon as piecing, couching, and embroidery beading.

It's okay to create tone-on-tone. Cross-locked beads, 1/4″ and 1/8″ ribbon couched onto handkerchief linen and a bag to match.

Designed for Statements debuting at the Kansas City Quilt Market, P & B Fabrics of browns and blacks was the challenge. The pieces in the ensemble included a basic black blouse; slacks with inset along the side seam; vest with couching, crinkling and beading; pieced belt; jacket of various embellishment techniques and piecing methods; and of course a handbag to match.

"Jack's Mardi Gras" vest began as a white crinkled fabric. Tumble Dyes and lots of thread, bead, and sequin couching created an entirely different look.

Different fabric combinations give surprising results. Personally I like bright and gaudy, however, sometimes less gaudy and less bright is nice, too.

Index